THE RIVALS
BLACKBURN *v.* BURNLEY

THE RIVALS

BLACKBURN *v.* BURNLEY

MIKE HOLGATE

TEMPUS

Frontispiece: Derby Doubles. Four internationals who played for both Burnley and Blackburn Rovers in a combined total of over 2,000 matches for the East Lancashire clubs. Clockwise from top right: Jack Bruton, Adam Blacklaw, John Connelly, Keith Newton.

First published 2005

Tempus Publishing Ltd
The Mill, Brimscombe Port
Stroud, Gloucestershire GL5 2QG
www.tempus-publishing.com

British Library Cataloguing in Publication Data.
A catalogue record for this book is available from the British Library.

ISBN 0 7524 2711 3

Typesetting and origination by Tempus Publishing
Printed and bound in Great Britain

Contents

Turf Moor, May 1991. STAYING DOWN 4 EVER LUV ROVERS HA HA HA. Highflying Rovers supporters taunt struggling Burnley as they head for elimination by lowly Torquay United in the second leg of a Division Four play-off semi-final.

Ewood Park, March 1913. Down to earth Burnley supporters wave a sympathetic message for Blackburn's skipper Bob Crompton. Defeat in this Sixth Round clash dashed the veteran's hopes of ever reaching an FA Cup final after Rovers had fallen at the semi-final stage during the two previous seasons.

Acknowledgements

The author is indebted to Blackburn photographer Howard Talbot, Burnley's official historian Ray Simpson, and soccer writer Norman Shields for providing many of the images. The various dream-team formations have been drawn together by the computer graphic skills of Ian Waugh. Thanks are also due to the staff of Burnley and Blackburn Libraries for contemporary match reports from the *Lancashire Evening Telegraph*, *Blackburn Evening Telegraph*, *Burnley Express* and *Blackburn Times*. Statistical information has been gleaned from *The PFA Premier & Football League Players' Records 1946-1998* plus annuals of the *Official PFA Footballers Factfile* (all edited by Barry J. Hugman); *Football League Tables 1888-1998* (edited by Michael Robinson); *History of Football* (by Mike Heatley & Ian Welch 1997); *Soccer at War* (by Jack Rollin 1985); *Burnley: A Complete Record 1882-1991* (by Edward Lee & Ray Simpson 1991); *The Essential History of Blackburn Rovers* (by Mike Jackman 2001); *Rothmans Football Yearbooks 1992-2002; History of the Lancashire Football Association 1878-1928* (compiled by Charles Sutcliffe and Fred Hargreaves 1928).

Introduction

In December 1957, the desire of a soccer-mad boy was realised when my father took me to watch my first football match. It was a 'friendly' between Burnley and Blackburn Rovers, to mark the inaugural game beneath floodlights at Turf Moor. Even closer to the action was the Burnley club mascot (my cousin David) and the referee R.P. Hartley (my headmaster at a local junior school). On a freezing cold night, with the pitch more suited to ice hockey, the ball bounced off the glistening white turf like a Barnes Wallis bomb, testing the ability of some of the greatest players ever to represent the clubs. On show for the Clarets were Colin McDonald, Jimmy McIlroy and Jimmy Adamson, while Rovers fielded Ronnie Clayton, Roy Vernon and Bryan Douglas – the scorer of the only goal of the game from the penalty spot. That season, Blackburn won promotion to join Burnley in the old First Division, which set up the prospect of more mouth-watering derbies for East Lancashire soccer fans. The best of these occurred in March 1960, when it was my painful privilege to witness a six-goal thriller in the sixth round of the FA Cup. Three down with seventeen minutes to go, Blackburn staged a miraculous recovery to equalise, then won the replay at Ewood Park in extra time. A month later my family moved to Devon as Burnley wrapped up the League Championship and ten-man Blackburn Rovers gamely finished runners-up to Wolves at Wembley. At that moment, it did not seem possible that these two proud clubs had both reached a peak from which they were to fall alarmingly – giving me the unexpected opportunity of watching them both in the lower reaches of the League as 'guests' of Torquay United. Thankfully, after decades in the wilderness, the fortunes of both clubs have improved dramatically. Their clash in Division One during the 2000/01 season was their first League meeting for seventeen years. While Premiership status still remains elusive for Burnley, hopefully they will soon renew their rivalry with Blackburn Rovers in the top flight – a sight not enjoyed by supporters since 1966 – the year of England's World Cup glory!

Mike Holgate
Torquay, May 2004

1

HAT-TRICK HEROES

Jack Southworth notched a record thirteen hat-tricks for Blackburn Rovers – starting with one in the first League derby against Burnley in 1888. This opening chapter salutes the marksmen who have accomplished this feat in competitive matches between the East Lancashire rivals.

FIRST DIVISION   3 NOVEMBER 1888
BURNLEY 1   BLACKBURN ROVERS 7
Attendance: 3,000

Founder members of the twelve-club Football League, Burnley and Blackburn squared up at Turf Moor desperate for points. After seven games of the inaugural season both clubs had won only two games, but it was the visitors who were to emerge as runaway victors in the first of many such League encounters.

A brave crowd endured miserable weather to witness this historic occasion and the visitors won the toss and chose to play with the wind and driving rain at their backs. Despite this disadvantage, the home side started brightly and brought the best out of Rovers' 'keeper Herbie Arthur who made some fine saves to deny the Burnley forwards. Blackburn's first goal-bound attempt was a fierce shot from half-back Jimmy Forrest which burst the ball! When play resumed, Beresford opened the scoring for Rovers after fifteen minutes and Forrest made up for his earlier disappointment by adding a second – a great individual effort, dribbling through the Burnley defence before slipping the ball past stand-in 'keeper Poland (normally a centre forward). Rovers increased their lead further through Herbert Fecitt before Burnley reduced the arrears with a headed goal from a winger making his debut for the club – Bill McKay. Burnley were disappointed when another effort was ruled offside. This was made all the more galling when the referee overruled their appeals for a similar offence when centre forward Jack Southworth ran through unchallenged and restored the three-goal cushion for Blackburn just before half-time. After the interval, the home side made valiant efforts to close the gap, but their luck was out. They enjoyed territorial advantage and won several corners but were unable to convert good opportunities into goals. With ten minutes to go, Rovers asserted their superiority and added three more goals before the final whistle, one from Fecitt and two from Jack Southworth who completed his hat-trick to inflict what is still Burnley's worst home defeat in an East Lancashire derby.

In the penultimate match of the season, Blackburn completed the double over ninth-placed Burnley who under Football League rules were then compelled to seek re-election. England international Jack Southworth bagged a brace in the 4-2 victory and emerged as Rovers' leading scorer with 21 League and FA Cup goals helping the club climb to a creditable fourth in the table. He emerged as one of the most prolific goalscorers of the fledgling League having begun his career alongside brother James at neighbours Blackburn Olympic – where he also regularly turned out in goal! Accumulating 121 goals in 132 League and cup appearances for Rovers, Jack also won two FA Cup winners' medals and 3 England caps. Apart from his obvious capabilities as a marksman, there were many other facets to Jack's game. Ball-winning tackles and passing

Jack Southworth.

skill allied to excellent close control and pace enabled him to create chances unselfishly for others. Five minutes from the end of a League encounter in December 1892, Jack clashed with Burnley defender Sandy Lang and both players were sent off. Having established an all-time record with a total of twelve goals in East Lancashire derbies, Jack moved to Everton in 1893 and became an instant legend on Merseyside for his goalscoring exploits. He struck a total of ten goals in two matches either side of Christmas notching 36 goals in 32 matches before injury abruptly ended his playing days. Luckily, he had another 'string to his bow' as a professional musician! Jack played violin for the Halle Orchestra and for thirty years was a member of the Pier Pavilion Orchestra in Llandudno.

Burnley (2-3-5)
F. Poland; Sandy Lang, Bill Bury; John Keenan, Dan Friel, J. Abrams; William McKay, Bob McCrae, William McFettridge, Jack Yates, Pat Gallocher.

Blackburn Rovers (2-3-5)
Herbie Arthur; James Southworth, John Forbes; Jimmy Douglas, Willie Almond, Jimmy Forrest; James Beresford, Nat Walton, Jack Southworth, Herbert Fecitt, Billy Townley. Secretary: Thomas Mitchell.

11

FIRST DIVISION   13 APRIL 1896
BURNLEY 6   BLACKBURN ROVERS 0
Attendance: 5,000

With both clubs comfortably placed in mid-table there was only local pride at stake in this end-of-season encounter at Turf Moor. Since the Football League had been formed in 1888, Burnley had won only three of fifteen derbies and suffered several drubbings at the hands of Blackburn. However, an improving Burnley side had lost by the only goal of the match at Ewood Park earlier in the season and were about to gain revenge by inflicting a heavy defeat on their rivals.

Played on Easter Monday, the match started at 5.30 p.m. and by half-time the size of the crowd had doubled as latecomers streamed into the ground after leaving work. Winning the toss, the home team elected to play with a stiff breeze at their backs and also had the benefit of a pronounced slope which then existed at Turf Moor. Blackburn did not put out their strongest side and chose the cauldron of this fixture to blood three youngsters. Centre half John Yarwood and inside forwards Parkinson and Whalley made their debuts while left-back Walter Porter was making only his third appearance of the season and was given a torrid time by Burnley right-winger Tom Nicol. The 'Turfites' opened their account only ten minutes into the game when a corner was converted by Walter Place senior. His son, Walter junior, playing on the left wing, hardly had a look in as Burnley mounted a wave of attacks along the right flank. Goalkeeper Adam Ogilvie was called upon to make smart saves from Nicol, Hill and McElney before Burnley extended their lead midway through the first half. Centre half Charles McElney sent a long ball out to the wing which Porter failed to clear. Latching onto the full-back's error, Tom Nicol cut inside and with only the 'keeper to beat made no mistake with a rasping shot. Rovers responded positively and the Burnley goal came briefly under pressure as 'keeper Willie Tatham had three shots to deal with. The visitors' hopes of a revival were rocked eight minutes before the interval when Nicol put his side further ahead after linking well with McEleny and Robertson. Drama followed when a goal-bound shot from James Hill was deflected by Porter's hand which almost deceived Ogilvie. The 'keeper reacted well to push the ball clear. The Burnley players believed the ball had crossed the line while the crowd appealed for a penalty, but the referee gave a free-kick on the edge of the box before blowing for half-time.

Even with the wind behind them in the second half, Rovers could not repel Burnley's rampant attack. Five minutes after the restart, Ogilvie failed to hold a shot from Hugh Robertson and the centre forward followed up to smash the ball into the net. Four minutes later, Walter Place jnr was brought into the game and showed what he was capable of by out-sprinting the defence and swinging over a cross which Nicol brilliantly volleyed into the roof of the net off the

Burnley 1896. Tom Nicol is pictured standing second from left in the back row.

underside of the bar for his hat-trick. The home side then relaxed slightly and allowed the visitors back into the game, but a resolute defence, in which full-back Jeremy Reynolds was outstanding, ensured that Willie Tatham was not troubled. With five minutes remaining, Nicol once more rounded Porter and whipped across a pinpoint cross which was headed home by Robertson to complete the rout. Tom Nicol's outstanding performance obviously impressed the hierarchy at Ewood Park, for by the following Christmas, a transfer bid was made and he was donning Rovers' colours. During that campaign Blackburn reasserted their dominance, completing the double over Burnley who had a nightmare season which resulted in relegation to the Second Division.

Burnley (2-3-5)
Willie Tatham; Jeremy Reynolds, Tom McLintock; Walter Place snr, Charles McEleny, Joe Taylor; Tom Nicol, Jim Hill, Hugh Robertson, Jim Davidson, Walter Place jnr. Secretary: Harry Bradshaw.

Blackburn Rovers (2-3-5)
Adam Ogilvie; Tom Brandon, Walter Porter; Gardner Hannah, John Yarwood, George Dewar; James Whitehead, James Parkinson, Josh Hargreaves, G. Whalley, Harry Chippendale. Secretary: Joseph Walmsley.

TEST MATCH   21 APRIL 1898
BLACKBURN ROVERS 1   BURNLEY 3
Attendance: 8,000

With no automatic promotion or relegation, an end-of-season series of Test Matches decided whether a club's future lay in the First or Second Division. In a season of contrasting fortunes for the East Lancashire rivals, Blackburn had finished above bottom club Stoke in the First Division, while Burnley had topped the Second Division ahead of Newcastle and only two of these four clubs could claim the right to occupy a place in the top flight the following season. Blackburn needed to make the most of home advantage in the first of two group matches with Burnley.

The much-vaunted derby produced a tame opening period, constantly interrupted by an over-officious referee who blew on numerous occasions for trivial offences. It was from one of these decisions that Rovers made a bizarre breakthrough after thirty-three minutes. Half-back Tom Booth took an indirect free-kick and Burnley 'keeper Jack Hillman made a grave mistake when he deliberately allowed the ball to pass him towards the net, which would have resulted in a goal kick being awarded, but he failed to notice winger Tom Briercliffe who popped up on the blindside to head the ball home. Five minutes after the interval, Rovers' 'keeper James Carter also made a costly error when he dropped a cross from Tom Morrison which was gratefully stabbed into the net by Wilf Toman who won a race for the ball with teammate Billy Bowes. This goal changed the whole face of the game and in the next attack the shaken 'keeper was beaten again in an aerial challenge allowing Toman to bundle the ball into the net and put the visitors ahead. The cross came once again from danger-man Tom Morrison, who recovered after slipping near the corner flag and kept the ball in play with his head as he lay on the floor. The winger started the move which enabled Wilf Toman to complete a hat-trick in fifteen minutes when he latched onto a cross from half-back David Beveridge to sew up the game for the Clarets. Rovers fought back gamely, but found Jack Hillman in peerless form, particularly with a one-handed save at full stretch to deny John Wilkie.

Wilf Toman was on the scoresheet again in the return at Turf Moor when Rovers were beaten 2-0. When the Test Matches involving Stoke and Newcastle were completed, Burnley were promoted, while Blackburn finished bottom of the group and faced the prospect of relegation – until they were saved by the Football League's decision to extend the number of clubs in the First Division, which meant that the Test Matches had all been a pointless exercise. Nevertheless, Burnley's coffers were swelled to the tune of £100 for beating Blackburn – a donation promised beforehand by former club president Mr C.J. Massey.

Born in Bishop Auckland in 1873, Wilf Toman joined Burnley from non-League Victoria United in December 1896. He made his League debut in the

Southampton 1901. Wilf Toman is seated second from the right in the middle row. Sitting on the end alongside him is former Blackburn and Burnley player Edgar Chadwick.

side which finished bottom of the First Division and failed to stave off relegation in the Test Matches. The following season he missed only one game as leader of the attack when the club bounced back and topped the Second Division. Having scored 35 goals in 74 games for the 'Turfites', Wilf was transferred to Everton in 1899 and two years later joined Southampton and was a prominent member of the Saints side which won the Southern League Championship.

Blackburn Rovers (2-3-5)
James Carter; Tom Brandon, Ted Killen; Tom Booth, Geordie Anderson, Harry Marshall; Tom Briercliffe, Ben Hulse, Josh Hargreaves, John Wilkie, John Campbell. Secretary: Joseph Walmsley.

Burnley (2-3-5)
Jack Hillman; Jeremy Reynolds, Tom McLintock; David Beveridge, Joseph Taylor, Archie Livingstone; Tom Morrison, Jimmy Ross, Wilf Toman, Billy Bowes, Walter Place jnr. Secretary: Harry Bradshaw.

FIRST DIVISION   28 NOVEMBER 1914

BLACKBURN ROVERS 6   BURNLEY 0

Attendance: 21,673

'Blackburn Rovers have at one time or another done some smart things at the expense of Burnley, but they eclipsed all their efforts on Sunday by inflicting a defeat by 6-0, which is the heaviest blow they have struck at Burnley at Ewood Park', admitted 'Sportsman' ruefully in the *Burnley Express*. This match was a clash of the East Lancashire titans as Blackburn and Burnley were the reigning Football League Champions and FA Cup holders respectively. Little went right for the visitors' inspirational captain Tommy Boyle, who lost the toss to his counterpart Bob Crompton, then spent most of the match carrying an injury following a challenge on the man he was marking, Percy Dawson. The Rovers' centre forward was in brilliant form and took full advantage by scoring four goals in a twenty-five minute spell during the first half.

The opening exchanges were fast and furious and both sides created chances before Percy Dawson put the home side ahead in the fourteenth minute when he beat left-back David Taylor and crashed a shot past his namesake Jerry Dawson in the Burnley goal. Seven minutes later Tommy Boyle received a leg injury and had to leave the field for treatment when he attempted to prevent Percy Dawson taking a pass from wing half Albert Walmsley to put Rovers two up. Boyle returned to play out the game as a limping passenger on the right wing. Burnley reshuffled their defence but could not hold the rampant Dawson who collected his hat-trick nine minutes before half-time when Tom Bamford failed to clear a cross from Jock Simpson and presented a simple chance which the striker gratefully tapped into the net. Burnley went close to reducing the arrears when Eddie Mosscrop's centre was palmed onto the crossbar by 'keeper Alf Robinson, but when Rovers resumed the attack Dawson headed in his fourth goal from an accurate cross from Joe Hodkinson.

Matters did not improve for the Clarets after the interval and six minutes after the restart a shot from Eddie Latherton was deflected past the 'keeper by luckless defender David Taylor. The Blackburn goal then survived two close shaves as a header by Walmsley bounced off the bar and Crompton cleared a free-kick off the line with Robinson beaten. Burnley's misery was completed with eight minutes remaining when they conceded a sixth goal scored by Eddie Latherton. Among the crowd were fifty wounded soldiers, casualties of the First World War, a conflict which would later claim the life of Blackburn's final scorer. A sad fact which puts the true importance of East Lancs derby 'battles' into perspective.

In the return at Turf Moor, Blackburn lost by the odd goal in five to finish third in the League – one place ahead of their rivals on goal difference. Percy Dawson was the club's leading scorer with 20 goals. The previous season he had made only a handful of appearances during the run-in to Blackburn's

Percy Dawson

Championship campaign. A big-money signing from Scottish club Heart of Midlothian, his potential was never fully realised as his career was to be severely curtailed by war. Two days after Percy's four goals had destroyed Burnley, the Football League management committee met in Manchester as it was now patently obvious that the First World War would not 'be over by Christmas'. Despite growing calls to abandon the game and encourage footballers to join other young men at the front, a decision was taken to carry on playing until the end of the season. By the time hostilities were over, Percy's best days were behind him but his goalscoring instinct had not deserted him and he continued to hit the net regularly until he left Ewood Park in 1923 – having notched 73 League and cup goals in 151 appearances.

Blackburn Rovers (2-3-5)

Alf Robinson; Bob Crompton, Arthur Cowell; Albert Walmsley, Percy Smith, Wattie Aitkenhead; Jock Simpson, Danny Shea, Percy Dawson, Eddie Latherton, Joe Hodkinson. Secretary: Robert Middleton.

Burnley (2-3-5)

Jerry Dawson; Tom Bamford, David Taylor; George Halley, Tommy Boyle, Billy Watson; Bob Kelly, Dick Lindley, Bert Freeman, Teddy Hodgson, Eddie Mosscrop. Secretary: John Haworth.

FOOTBALL LEAGUE	6 OCTOBER 1917
LANCASHIRE SECTION	
BURNLEY 6	BLACKBURN ROVERS 1
Attendance: 1,000	

Due to the fluctuating availability of players in wartime, both clubs made several changes from the teams that had faced each other a week earlier at Ewood Park. Rovers had gained their first points of the season by inflicting a 3-1 defeat on their derby rivals. The Clarets exacted swift revenge in the return through the introduction of former England centre forward Bert Freeman whose goalscoring pedigree was the crucial difference between the two sides. When the Football League had been suspended for the duration, players who were not called up for the armed forces had to find other means of livelihood as the *Burnley Express* reported in the case of 'Freeman, who is showing loyalty to the club in a distinctly praiseworthy fashion, for, having business within easy range of the Brunside town, he is treating the club very generously in the matter of expenses when assisting'.

Winning the toss, the home side chose to play towards the Beehole End with a strong breeze at their backs. In the opening attack of the game, Bert Freeman rose above the Rovers defence and thudded a header against the upright, but quickly got his name on the scoresheet in the seventh minute when he broke through a tackle and drove the ball in off a post. Midway through the first half, Blackburn 'keeper Gaskell kicked clear a ball which was volleyed straight back past him by Heslop standing just inside the penalty area. Ten minutes before the interval, the Burnley wing half made a third goal when his cross was met on the half-volley by Freeman who rifled in a shot off the underside of the bar.

A determined Rovers team came out fighting in the second half and reduced the arrears in the seventy-third minute when centre forward Mart headed home a corner. Within four minutes, Burnley regained their three-goal advantage when Woods scored from an acute angle after the winger's first effort had been parried by Gaskell. Freeman then collected his hat-trick in a demonstration of his class. Collecting the ball out wide on the left wing, he cut in and dribbled towards goal, eluding three challenges before firing past the helpless Gaskell. Freeman then turned provider, setting up Woodward for Burnley's sixth goal and their first victory of the season in six games! At the end of the campaign, Blackburn finished last of sixteen teams in the Lancashire Section of the wartime League with their East Lancashire rivals just one place above them.

Bert Freeman was already an international when he arrived at Turf Moor in 1911. After spells with Aston Villa and Arsenal he made his reputation at Everton where he was the Football League's leading scorer with 36 goals in 1909, when the Toffees finished runners-up in the First Division. At the peak of his form, he provided the vital cutting edge to a fine Burnley side who were

Bert Freeman

now ready to challenge for the top honours. The Clarets won promotion from the Second Division with Bert contributing 31 goals in 37 games. The following season, he scored the only goal of the match as Burnley beat Liverpool at Crystal Palace to lift the FA Cup for the only time in their history. Bert played for England on three more occasions while at Turf Moor, and when the Football League was resumed after the First World War, he became the first Burnley player to score 100 League goals as the club finished runners-up in the race for the title in 1920. The veteran striker was to miss out when the club went one better a year later. After a disastrous start, losing the first three matches of the campaign, Bert lost his place in the side. Old Father Time had crully caught up with the prolific marksman just as Burnley embarked on a glorious thirty match unbeaten run to clinch the League Championship.

Burnley (2-3-5)
J. Quinn; Billy Nesbitt, Henry Hastie; Dick Lindley, M. Duxbury, T. Heslop; E. Woods, B. Edwards, Bert Freeman, F. Woodward, G. Johnson.

Blackburn Rovers (2-3-5)
A. Gaskell; T. Atherton, J. Waters; W. Duckworth, James Boothman, S. Baker; R. McArthur, D. Moorcroft, J. Mart, J. Lucas, F. Forshaw.

FOOTBALL LEAGUE   12 OCTOBER 1918
LANCASHIRE SECTION
BLACKBURN ROVERS 3   BURNLEY 4
Attendance: 1,500

A month before the Armistice signalled the end of the First World War, Burnley had the services of Sergeant-Major Wilcox, Gunner Hastie and Corporal Grant as both sides made four changes from the teams that had played at Ewood Park a week earlier when the home side had won by the only goal of the game. The result gained Rovers their first win of the season and left fellow strugglers Burnley with no points from five matches. The return was to prove just as close but on this occasion seven goals were scored in a 'ding-dong' encounter which provided thrilling entertainment for the terrace critics who described it as the best match of the season.

Blackburn 'keeper Gaskell was called into action within minutes of the start and made a brave save at the feet of Dick Lindley. Moments later, the Burnley wing half broke through the defence again and passed to Bert Freeman who took the chance well to open the scoring. Rovers quickly levelled when the ball broke to Boothman from a scrimmage and his snap shot went in off the inside of the upright. The visitors stormed back and regained the advantage when a cross from Grant was headed home by Freeman. Burnley 'keeper Wilcox was enjoying a spot of Army leave and made two excellent saves before he was beaten by Rushton after fine work by Levers. Centre forward Bert Freeman then notched his third with a goal remarkably similar to the one he had scored to collect a derby hat-trick the previous season. Finding space by dropping deep, he picked up the ball on the halfway line and his pace took him past three defenders before he effortlessly planted the ball in the net for the best goal of the game. Yet again, Rovers came from behind to equalise before the interval. Finney was adjudged to have fouled Boothman and Levers made no mistake from the penalty spot.

Soon after the resumption, Freeman provided the chance for inside right Cunningham to restore the visitors' lead. The crowd must have wondered what more fireworks were in store, but the home side were unable to respond with wing half Duckworth leaving the field for ten minutes to receive treatment to an injury. When he returned it was as a limping passenger, making up the numbers out on the left wing. The Clarets were unable to take full advantage of Rovers' plight and were lucky when Rushton squandered an excellent chance to snatch an equaliser by slicing the ball wide of an open goal. The luckless centre forward did not get another opportunity to score as he was switched to full-back when Brandon also picked up an injury to further incapacitate the home side. Burnley held on to their slender lead to register their first victory and by the end of the campaign Blackburn were propping up the table for the second consecutive season.

Bert Freeman

Bert Freeman was Burnley's top scorer with 19 goals in 31 games but passed his peak during the First World War years. Aged 35, he played little part in the League Championship triumph of 1921 and at the end of the season he moved on to Wigan Borough having scored 115 goals in 166 official League and cup games for Burnley. Measuring only 5' 8" tall, Bert could not employ the robust tactics of many of his contemporaries and his formidable goal tally was gained through an intelligent ability to lead the attack with skill and finesse which also created goalscoring opportunities for his colleagues.

Blackburn Rovers (2-3-5)
A. Gaskell; T. Brandon, J. Birmingham; W. Duckworth, James Boothman, O. Ralph; W. Levus, F. Livesey, H. Rushton, H. Rothwell, R Haworth.

Burnley (2-3-5)
J. Wilcox; W. Finney, W. Newton; Henry Hastie, Dick Lindley, A. Newton; B. Grant, G. Cunningham, Bert Freeman, J. Cowgill, J. Clarkson.

FIRST DIVISION   13 SEPTEMBER 1924

BURNLEY 3   BLACKBURN ROVERS 5

Attendance: 16,000

Blackburn made several changes from the side which had been beaten by four goals at Newcastle three days earlier. Manager John Haworth must have wondered what else he could do to improve the side when the derby set off at a cracking pace and Burnley tore the Rovers' defence to shreds – completely overwhelming the visitors to go three goals up in the first fifteen minutes! However, inspired by the performance of inside forward John McIntyre, the blue and whites staged the greatest comeback in the history of this derby fixture to emerge as comfortable victors.

Facing driving rain did not deter the home side who tore into the opposition from the start and centre forward George Beel wasted a golden chance in the first attack by tamely shooting straight at Ronnie Sewell. This was a temporary respite for Burnley's former 'keeper as he conceded three goals in five minutes. Ronnie got both hands to the ball but failed to stop a piledriver from Jack 'Ginger' Hill. The red-haired centre half then came up for a corner and added a second goal by heading home a George Waterfield corner before the same winger jinked past two defenders and swung over a cross which was headed in firmly by centre forward Albert Freeman. Burnley seemed home and dry despite the fact that John McIntyre quickly created an opportunity for Jock McKay to pull one back for Blackburn, but the course of the match was changed by two controversial incidents which occurred shortly before the interval. Beel thought he had restored his side's three-goal lead but was adjudged offside before the well-placed referee infuriated the home fans even further by ruling that a left-foot shot from John McIntyre had crossed the line after bouncing down off the underside of the crossbar.

There was no doubt that Rovers had struck a psychological blow and came out for the second half with renewed confidence. Anxiety overtook the Burnley team when good work by McIntyre put right-winger Joe Hulme through for the equaliser in the fifty-fourth minute. Ten minutes later, George Beel made a hash of an attempted back-pass which McIntyre intercepted to round Burnley's 'keeper and put his side ahead by slipping the ball into an unguarded net. Burnley pivot Jack Hill was cruelly exposed as he manfully attempted to stem the tide as the Blackburn attack tore holes in the home defence. Inevitably the visitors cemented their lead with ten minutes left as John McIntyre made certain of the result with a goal to clinch his hat-trick. The delight of the visiting suppoters was summed up by a reporter in the *Blackburn Times*: 'A win over Burnley has always been sufficient to create enthusiasm and revitalise flagging interest, but to beat Burnley men on their own field when the Rovers were three goals down [...] was a splendid performance and a very gallant feat, [...] some hundreds of Blackburn people [...] experienced every emotion of the

John McIntyre

football spectator – from the uneasy conviction that Burnley were going to win easily, to feeling of hope, then glorious certainty that there was a chance after all, and finally realisation which could only be expressed by making as much noise as possible.' It came as no surprise when the visitors cemented their lead with ten minutes left as John McIntyre made certain of the result with a goal which delighted the visiting supporters and clinched his hat-trick.

Glasgow-born John McIntyre had been signed from Sheffield Wednesday in 1922 and immediately impressed by hitting four goals in five minutes against Everton. Yet, in six seasons at Ewood Park his main role was that of a midfield schemer and he collected only 38 goals in 194 League and cup appearances. Later converted to the wing, then wing half as he reached the veteran stage, John played only two games in season 1927/28 before moving on to end his career at Blackpool during Blackburn's FA Cup-winning campaign.

Burnley (2-3-5)
Jerry Dawson; Len Smelt, Jim Evans; Alf Bassnett, Jack Hill, George Parkin; Bob Kelly, Benny Cross, George Beel, Albert Freeman, George Waterfield.
Manager: John Haworth.

Blackburn Rovers (2-3-5)
Ron Sewell; Bob Roxburgh, Tom Wylie; Jack Roscamp, Harry Healless, Aussie Campbell; Joe Hulme, Jock McKay, Ted Harper, John McIntyre, Jack Crisp.
Manager: Jack Carr.

FIRST DIVISION   31 OCTOBER 1925
BURNLEY 1   BLACKBURN ROVERS 3
Attendance: 26,181

'Sportsman', writing in the *Blackburn Times*, commented how times had changed from the recent past when Rovers' visits to Turf Moor were viewed rather 'like David tackling Goliath'. Burnley's captain during those heady days after the First World War was Tommy Boyle who had joined the coaching staff and was drafted in as a replacement linesman for this game. The referee allowed the match go ahead despite foggy conditions that made smokers' matches appear like beacons as members of the crowd lit their cigarettes. Unfortunately for the home fans, their team failed to 'shine' in the same way as this derby defeat left them in trouble near the bottom of the table with only two wins in fourteen League games! Burnley had been hammered 10-0 by Aston Villa in the opening game of the season and came into the derby having suffered a 8-3 beating at Manchester City the previous Saturday.

After experiencing a calamitous start to the season, it was something of a relief for supporters of the Clarets that there was no score in the match against their close neighbours by the time the teams trooped off the field at the interval. Rovers' prolific goalscorer Ted Harper had been making the most of changes introduced to the offside law that season but against Burnley seemed to be having one of those games where nothing would go right. Centre half Jack Hill's job was made easy for him as Ted's first touch frequently let him down, but his unquenchable spirit and determination was to transform his team's fortunes in the second half.

The turning point of the match came when Blackburn snatched the lead after 62 minutes. Harper latched onto a ball twenty-five yards out. On this occasion he didn't bother trying to control the ball, but hit it first time – driving an unstoppable shot past helpless 'keeper Jerry Dawson. Burnley strove hard for the equaliser but were frequently denied by the flying brilliance of 'keeper Jock Crawford. Suddenly, with six minutes left, there was a goal-rush sparked by Ted Harper who bravely put his side two up with a bullet header to reach a cross from Joe Hulme and three minutes later the winger beat the defence again to set up Harper for his hat-trick. To their credit, Burnley hit back with a terrific cross-shot from winger Louis Page which beat Crawford all ends up. The 'keeper did well to prevent the same player from repeating the trick moments later and was fortunate in the last minute when inside forward Benny Cross somehow pulled his shot wide of an open goal with the last kick of the match.

Blackburn's hat-trick hero earned this praise from 'Sportsman': 'Harper in general was too unhappy with the ball to have one of his best days in a pure football sense. But his pluck and driving power, and his felicity when he gets a ball moving towards him near goal, are inestimably precious to the side'. The striker established a club record, finishing the season with a staggering 43 goals

Ted Harper

from only 37 League games and in two spells for Rovers, amassed 122 goals in 177 League and cup matches. The centre forward scored on his debut for Rovers in 1923 but with limited footballing skills, failed to establish himself as a regular in the first team. All that changed in September 1925 when he was brought into the side and hammered five goals in an away match against Newcastle. His hat-trick against Burnley brought his tally to an incredible 19 goals in 11 matches and by the end of the season he had been selected for England. This proved to be Ted's only international appearance but he continued to serve Blackburn well until his goalscoring ability took him to Sheffield Wednesday, Tottenham and Preston before ending his playing days back at Ewood Park, where he continued for many years on the coaching staff.

Burnley (2-3-5)
Jerry Dawson; Andy McCluggage, George Waterfield; Alf Bassnett, Jack Hill, Len Hughes; Jack Bruton, Benny Cross, Bob Kelly, George Beel, Louis Page.
Manager: Albert Pickles.

Blackburn Rovers (2-3-5)
Jock Crawford; David Rollo, Bob Roxburgh; Jack Roscamp, Harry Healless, Aussie Campbell; Joe Hulme, Syd Puddefoot, Ted Harper, John McIntyre, Arthur Rigby.
Manager: Jack Carr.

FIRST DIVISION   13 MARCH 1926

BLACKBURN ROVERS 6   BURNLEY 3

Attendance: 29,991

The *Blackburn Times* described this classic derby as a 'feast to suit the most fastidious, and will make the contest one to be remembered in the annals of the meetings of the two clubs'. Relegation-haunted Burnley suffered their second defeat of the season at the hands of Rovers. Danger-man Ted Harper had scored Blackburn's three goals at Turf Moor, but on this occasion only managed to get on the scoresheet once. Syd Puddefoot scored twice and it was Arthur Rigby's turn to help himself to a hat-trick against the struggling Clarets. Blackburn themselves were not out of the woods having suffered from inconsistent form and in fact ended the season only five points above Burnley. Although the Rovers' goalscoring machine hit the net 91 times during the League campaign, this was only six more goals than their East Lancashire rivals who finished third from bottom and avoided relegation by a single point!

Missing from the derby line-up were first choice centre halves Harry Healless of Blackburn and Jack Hill of Burnley who had both been selected for the Football League to face the Scottish League. Their defensive qualities were sorely missed as eight of the nine goals were scored during an incredible 15-minute spell in the second-half after an undistinguished first period when Blackburn had gone into the interval holding a slender one-goal lead – courtesy of a close-range header by inside forward Syd Puddefoot. Defences remained on top for a further half-hour after the break until an avalanche commenced with two goals in two minutes from Arthur Rigby and Syd Puddefoot respectively. This burst should have sewn up the game for Rovers but the visitors immediately opened their account through inside right Percy Richards, before Rigby responded by extending the home side's lead with two quick goals to collect his hat-trick with just ten minutes remaining. With a valiant late rally, winger Jack Bruton reduced the arrears, then Percy Richards bagged his second, bringing the score back to respectability for the Clarets. Blackburn supporters may have had visions of a repetition of a game against Birmingham a few weeks earlier when the team had squandered a winning lead before having to be content with a 4-4 draw, but with three minutes left, Blackburn's top scorer Ted Harper had the last word, hitting his side's sixth goal to complete the rout. Despite relaxing their grip on the game, Blackburn had won with plenty to spare and the defeat would have been even more comprehensive had it not been for a fantastic display of goalkeeping from Burnley veteran Jerry Dawson, who could not be blamed for any of his side's defensive lapses. Playing in what proved to be his last derby, he produced his best save in the last minute to deny Syd Puddefoot from also claiming a hat-trick when he turned away a tremendous drive to bring the game to a thrilling finale.

Arthur Rigby

The difference between the two sides was highlighted by the *Blackburn Times*: 'The Rovers were blessed with two great inside forwards in Puddefoot and Rigby. The first-named schemed spendidly all through the game and it was quite fitting he should score the only goal of the first half. Afterwards Rigby was quite his equal and displayed fine, forceful football with deadly shooting.' Arthur Rigby arrived from Bradford City in 1925 and established himself as an exciting left-winger of international class, winning 5 England caps during his time at Ewood Park. As in the game against Burnley when he collected a hat-trick, he was often switched to inside forward but lined up for Blackburn on the flank when the club won the 1928 FA Cup final. After one more season at Ewood Park, Arthur moved on to Everton, who became Second Division Champions in 1931, before his career petered out at Middlesbrough, Clapton Orient and Crewe Alexandra. The skilful ball-playing forward with a powerful shot scored 44 goals in 168 League and cup games for Rovers.

Blackburn Rovers (2-3-5)

Ron Sewell; David Rollo, Herbert Jones; Jimmy McKinnell, Aussie Campbell, John McIntyre; Jack Crisp, Syd Puddefoot, Ted Harper, Arthur Rigby, Tom Mitchell. Manager: Albert Pickles.

Burnley (2-3-5)

Jerry Dawson; Andy McCluggage, George Waterfield; John Steel, Steve Spargo, Billy Dougall; Jack Bruton, Percy Richards, Bill Roberts, George Beel, Louis Page. Manager: Jack Carr.

FIRST DIVISION   9 NOVEMBER 1929
BLACKBURN ROVERS 8   BURNLEY 3
Attendance : 22, 647

Both sides had key men absent from their line-ups for this memorable derby clash. Rovers were missing skipper Harry Healess, Syd Puddefoot and Arthur Rigby, while Burnley were without Harry Storer and Sam Wadsworth. All five players were England internationals, yet the crowd who braved miserable weather to attend the game were treated to the highest scoring East Lancs League derby of all time.

A few weeks earlier, Blackburn had beaten Birmingham 7-5, which was seen as a freak result as the Midlands side had been hampered by a serious injury to their England goalkeeper Harry Hibbs. By an amazing coincidence this derby was also marred when the visitors' goalkeeper Billy Down played much of the game in pain. On the team's return to Burnley, he was rushed to hospital where he was diagnosed to be suffering from a ruptured kidney. However, the unfortunate 'keeper could do nothing to prevent Rovers' opener when inside forward Arthur Groves shrugged off a crunching challenge to open the scoring with a fierce drive after twenty-five minutes. Down was then injured after colliding heavily with onrushing winger Wilf Crompton, but bravely resumed between the posts after receiving treatment to his back from the trainer's 'magic sponge'. A foul on Burnley winger Jack Bruton gave Andy McCluggage a chance to equalise from the spot and the full-back made no mistake with the penalty kick. Blackburn restored the lead shortly before half-time when leader of the attack Jack Roscamp headed home a pinpoint centre from left-winger Ted Turner. Seven minutes after the interval, Roscamp unwittingly increased the home side's lead when Down attempted to clear the ball which rebounded off the centre forward's body into the net. Within five minutes the Burnley defence was breached twice more with spectacular goals. The first of these was a twenty-five-yard screamer from Tommy McLean who hit the ball into the top corner of the net as he tumbled over from the weight of a challenge. Joe Imrie then scored his first goal for Blackburn with a free-kick on the edge of the area awarded for a foul on Jack Roscamp. The visitors bravely fought back and reduced the arrears when Bruton cleverly beat full-back Bert Jones and pulled the ball back into the path of Louis Page who beat 'keeper Jock Crawford from close range. A mistake by Down allowed a shot from McLean to slip through his outstretched hands for Rovers' sixth goal. The goal feast continued when a move by Roscamp and Turner produced a simple chance which was tapped in by Groves before McCluggage scored his second penalty for Burnley after Jones had clearly handled. The eleventh and final goal of the match came in the last minute when Groves completed the rout and celebrated a hat-trick.

Sitting in the stand were two FA selectors who reportedly had come to run the rule over Rovers' new goalscoring sensation Arthur Groves. Having been

Arthur Groves

signed from Halifax, his hat-trick against Burnley brought his tally to 10 goals in 10 League matches, yet international recognition never materialised. He made only six more first-team appearances that season and did not add to his tally as Syd Puddefoot and Tommy McLean were preferred at inside forward. Arthur never became an automatic choice during his stay at Ewood Park and after scoring 26 goals in 68 League and cup appearances for Rovers moved on to Derby in 1933. As a scout for Luton Town, he recommended his own son to manager Dally Duncan who later took over at Ewood Park. That same season, wing half John Groves played for the Hatters in the 1959 FA Cup final.

Blackburn Rovers (2-3-5)
Jock Crawford; Jock Hutton, Herbert Jones; Bill Imrie, Bill Rankin, Peter O'Dowd; Wilf Crompton, Tommy McLean, Jack Roscamp, Arthur Groves, Ted Turner. Honorary Manager: Bob Crompton.

Burnley (2-3-5)
Billy Down; Andy McCluggage, George Waterfield; Jim Brown, Stan Bowsher, John Steel; Jack Bruton, Jim Wallace, Joe Mantle, Joe Devine, Louis Page. Manager: Albert Pickles.

FOOTBALL LEAGUE NORTH   19 FEBRUARY 1944
ALSO FOOTBALL LEAGUE WAR CUP QUALIFYING COMPETITION

BURNLEY 5   BLACKBURN ROVERS 1

Attendance: 7,107

During the Second World War, clubs 'soldiered on' with a mix of amateur and professional players participating in regional Leagues with different competitions held either side of Christmas. In season 1943/44, fifty clubs competed in the first competition and Blackburn finished twelfth, twelve places above Burnley. The second competition attracted fifty-six clubs and this derby at Turf Moor also served as a qualifying match for the Football League War Cup which Blackburn Rovers had won in 1940.

The previous week, a derby at Ewood Park had resulted in a convincing 3-1 win for Burnley. In the return, Rovers could not contain the Clarets' lively forward line and the home side took full advantage to improve their goal average whenever the opposing defence faltered. The spearhead of the attack, Bob Brocklebank, helped himself to a first-half hat-trick. He put his side ahead in the seventh minute, latching onto a mistake by his marker Bob Pryde who failed to clear. The Rovers had started the game with ten men, but were then bolstered by the late appearance of wing half Arnold Whiteside. Brocklebank extended the home team's lead after fourteen minutes, converting a lob from Geddes after a throw-in by Rudman. Eight minutes before half-time Brocklebank scored his third, a magnificent solo effort culminating in a thirty-yard high drive which beat the despairing dive of 'keeper Conway. Six minutes after the interval, Brocklebank turned provider when he touched on a centre from Sargent into the path of Watson who made no mistake from close range. Burnley's fifth goal came in the sixty-fifth minute when Brocklebank took his personal goal tally to four when he gathered a cross from Sargent and deceived the 'keeper with a swerving shot. The Clarets relaxed and sat on their lead allowing Rovers back into the game. Shortly before the close, the visitors scored a consolation goal when unmarked right-winger Aspden converted a cross from Guest on the opposite flank.

Burnley's match-winner received special praise from the sports correspondent of the *Burnley Express*, 'Brocklebanks leadership has never been better'. Bob Brocklebank spent six years with Aston Villa before joining Burnley in March 1936. A stylish inside forward, he immediately lined up in the Burnley side alongside goalscoring sensation Tommy Lawton. The immaculately turned-out player was nicknamed 'The Toff' by supporters and in the period before the Second World War, Bob scored 38 League and cup goals in 128 appearances for the Clarets. During the summer months, Bob's talent as a cricketer also made him a popular captain of Lancashire League club Lowerhouse. Although at the veteran stage, he continued to turn out regularly in wartime matches for Burnley and in 1945 was appointed manager of

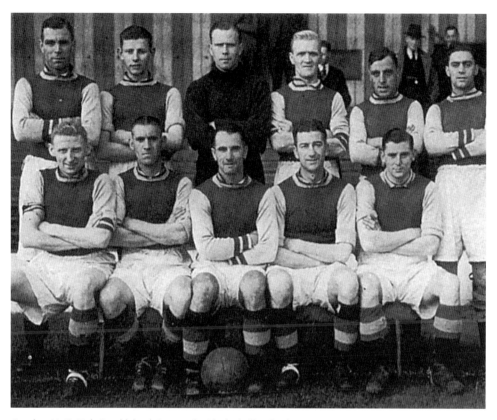

Burnley 1943. Bob Brocklebank is seated with the ball at his feet.

Birmingham. After six years at St Andrews he moved onto similar posts at Hull City and Bradford City before leaving the game in 1964. A versatile forward who could fill the role of midfield schemer or leader of the attack, he was one of those unfortunate players who was overlooked for possible international honours by reaching their peak during the Second World War years.

Burnley (2-3-5)
Jimmy Strong; D. Geddes, Harold Mather; Harold Rudman, Arthur Woodruff, C. Webster; Tom Gardner, F. Reid, Bob Brocklebank, D. Watson, H. Sargent.

Blackburn Rovers (2-3-5)
H. Conway; W. Taylor, Walter Crook; Arnold Whiteside, Bob Pryde, W. Robertson; T. Aspden, Jackie Wharton, Jimmy Dougal, Harry Stephan, Billy Guest.

FOOTBALL LEAGUE NORTH   27 OCTOBER 1945
BURNLEY 1   BLACKBURN ROVERS 4
Attendance: 7,964

Although the Second World War was over, many soccer players in the armed services were still waiting for demobilisation and football continued with a regional format. The Football League North contained twenty-two teams and in the first meeting of the East Lancashire rivals, Blackburn won 4-2 at Ewood Park, with 'guest player' Cecil Wyles scoring for the home side. The return, a week later, was to be a personal triumph for the centre forward who had completed a transfer from Everton in midweek and he had celebrated with a nap hand of goals for his new club. The result left Burnley still searching for their first home win of the season and the reason was partly explained by 'Sportsman' in the *Burnley Express*: 'One does not always believe in "hard luck" stories to excuse a Burnley defeat [...] but the way in which decisions have gone against them in recent matches is becoming too monotonous to escape attention'.

Shrugging off their recent poor form, the home side sparkled and totally dominated the first half-hour. They took the lead in the thirteenth minute when their centre forward Hold shook off two defenders and scored with a glorious drive into the top corner of the net. Against the run of play, Rovers levelled the scores before half-time when they were awarded a penalty for handball which was converted by Wyles.

In the first Rovers attack after the interval, full-back Harold Mather miskicked a clearance against Hall who quickly controlled the ball and the winger crossed for Wyles to put the visitors ahead. Minutes later, the centre forward completed his 'hat-trick' after nodding home a corner. The referee incensed the home supporters with three controversial decisions in the second half. The official turned down two appeals for a penalty, the first after a handling offence by a Rovers defender and the second when left-winger Peter Kippax had his legs whipped from under him in a challenge. There was uproar behind the Rovers' goal and play had to be held up after a goal attempt was disallowed when 'keeper Jim Barron mishandled and appeared to let the ball cross the line before snatching it back. Burnley's luck was out and when calm was restored they became thoroughly disheartened when the visitors stretched their lead still further with a magnificent thirty-yard drive by Cecil Wyles which was by far the best goal of the match. The shot was so powerful that Burnley's new 'keeper Jack Breedon injured himself trying to stop it! Blackburn had completed an early season double over Burnley but ended the season second from bottom with their neighbours improving to finish five places above them.

Cecil 'Barney' Wyles finished the season as Blackburn's top scorer with 17 goals from 24 League and cup games but never made an official Football League appearance for the club. At the end of the season, the twenty-six-year-old striker

Cecil Wyles

was transferred to Bury where he made his long-awaited League debut for the 'Shakers', but after only one more game moved on to Southport where he became a cult hero notching 53 goals in 143 League games before ending his League career with the Third Division (North) club in 1950. As a youngster, he had been an England schoolboy international at centre half but was converted into a bustling centre forward when signed by Everton in February 1938. The following season the Merseyside club won the League Championship while Cecil learned his craft in the reserves who succeeded in lifting the Central League Championship. It was the last League campaign before the Second World War which prevented him from challenging for a place in the first team. Despite scoring three hat-tricks whilst crashing in 23 goals in 18 matches for the Toffees in season 1944/45, he was released to join Blackburn and there is little doubt that wartme seriously curtailed the striker's development as a possible sucessor to Goodison Park's great England, and former Burnley, centre forward Tommy Lawton.

Burnley (2-3-5)

Jack Breedon; D. Mulvaney, Harold Mather; T. Wilson, Arthur Woodruff, Harold Rudman; Jack Hays, Tom Gardner, O. Hold, D. Meek, Peter Kippax.
Manager: Cliff Britton.

Blackburn Rovers (2-3-5)

Jim Barron; Walter Crook, Alan Green; George Glaister, George Forbes, Eric Bell; W. Hall, Billy Rogers, Cecil Wyles, Harry Stephan, Jackie Campbell.

EAST LANCASHIRE HAT-TRICK RECORDS

Above left: Blackburn-born Burnley forward Jack Yates scored a hat-trick on his debut for England in their 6-1 defeat of Ireland in 1889. Amazingly, he was never selected for international duty again!

Above right: Winger Billy Townley became the first player to score a hat-trick in an FA Cup final when Blackburn Rovers beat Sheffield Wednesday 6-1 at the Kennington Oval during the first 'War of the Roses' final in 1890.

Above left: England 1966 World Cup squad member John Connelly is the only player to have scored a League hat-trick for both Burnley and Blackburn Rovers.

Above right: In the 1920s and early 1930s, goal-machine George Beel hit a record eleven hat-tricks for Burnley as he was top scorer for six seasons. His best total of 35 League goals in a season, and career aggregate of 187 goals for the club, also remain unbeaten.

2

CUP CLASHES

Patient fans queue outside Ewood Park hoping to obtain tickets for the FA Cup sixth-round derby replay in March 1960.

LANCASHIRE CUP FINAL 26 APRIL 1890
BURNLEY 2 BLACKBURN ROVERS 0
Attendance: 15,000

A month before this shock result, Blackburn Rovers lifted the FA Cup and that season had also completed a League 'double' over their derby rivals. Burnley had never come close to getting their hands on the 'Palatine Pot', whereas Rovers had reached seven of the previous ten finals making them overwhelming favourites with the bookies. This was not surprising as Burnley faced re-election after finishing second from bottom in the League, despite an improvement in form which left them unbeaten in their last five games. Blackburn had in fact, been the last team to beat Burnley in the League and lined up against them in this clash with eight of the players from their triumphant FA Cup side.

The Lancashire Cup final was played at the Thorneyholme Road ground of Accrington FC where souvenirs of the occasion were on sale. One Blackburn vendor proudly proclaimed that two individual portraits of his favourites were worth the price of the entire opposition team being offered on a presentation plate by the publishers of the *Burnley Express*. Turfites skipper Sandy Lang won the toss and chose to play with the wind and his team attacked aggressively from the start. After several close shaves, Rovers broke out of defence and winger Joe Lofthouse shook off a foul challenge by Lang to score. Unluckily, the goal was disallowed as the referee had blown to award a free-kick to Rovers. Burnley pressed forward again and took the lead after half an hour. Good combination play between Claude Lambie and James Hill set up a clear-cut chance for inside left Alex Stewart. Shortly after the interval, Burnley winger Bob Haresnape had to leave the field temporarily for treatment to an injury. This did nothing to slow down the remaining ten men and Rovers had another scare when centre forward Claude Lamble found the net – only for the goal to be disallowed for offside. Blackburn gradually fought their way back into the game and upped the tempo considerably, creating chance after chance. The fact that they did not equalise was down to the outstanding form of Burnley 'keeper Archie Kaye, who made a string of brilliant saves to deny the Rovers' attack. With fifteen minutes remaining, Burnley sewed up the match when a fierce drive from Hill rebounded off the bar, Stewart's follow-up shot was blocked before inside right Alex McLardie forced the ball over the line for his side's second goal. Towards the end, disappointed Rovers fans standing on the touchlines began to encroach upon the pitch, but their unsporting behavior could not affect the result. Ecstatic Burnley supporters responded by singing a chorus of 'There'll be no more sorrow there' and when the final whistle sounded, they surged forward to carry hero Archie Kaye shoulder high from the field of play.

The *Athletic News* reported: 'I never saw the Blackburn Rovers better beaten than they were in the Lancashire final on Saturday. Burnley overplayed them in

The triumphant Burnley team pose with the Lancashire Cup (the 'Palatine Pot').

every direction, and one could hardly believe that we had the winners of the English Cup fighting such an hopeless battle.' These sentiments were echoed when the victorious team returned to a rapturous reception in Burnley. Riding in a waggonette proceeded by the Volunteer Band playing such sterling tunes as *See the Conquering Hero Come* and *Truth 'til Death*, the team stopped for well-earned refreshments at the Bull Hotel. There, a proud committee member made a rousing speech proclaiming that, having defeated the English cup-holders, the Burnley club could not only claim to be the best team in Lancashire, but had earned the right to be recognised as the 'champion team in England'.

Burnley (2-3-5)
Archie Kaye; Bill Bury, Sandy Lang; Bill McFetridge, Daniel Spiers, Jack Keenan; Bob Haresnape, Alex McCardle, Claude Lambie, Alex Stewart, James Hill.
Secretary: Edward White.

Blackburn Rovers (2-3-5)
Jack Horne; Tom Brandon, John Forbes; John Barton, George Dewar, Willie Almond; Joe Lofthouse, Henry Campbell, John Southworth, Nat Walton, Billy Townley.
Secretary: Thomas Mitchell.

FA CUP FOURTH ROUND   8 MARCH 1913

BLACKBURN ROVERS 0   BURNLEY 1

Attendance: 42,778

The outcome of the toss was crucial and when Burnley skipper Tommy Boyle called correctly, he condemned his counterpart Bob Crompton to face a stiff breeze. Both men had cruel experiences of the FA Cup. Three years previously, Tommy Boyle had collected a losers' medal as captain of Barnsley, while long-serving Bob Crompton had never fulfilled his dream to lift the trophy for his hometown club. With Rovers hoping to reach their third semi-final in a row, the moment was not lost on humorous Clarets supporters who carried a sympathetic banner proclaiming: 'THE PARTING OF THE WAYS – IT'S HARD LUCK BOB BUT WE'VE GOT TO DO IT' (see page 6). With home advantage, reigning League Champions Rovers were expected to beat their Second Division neighbours comfortably. Both clubs had players with injury problems during the build-up to the match but announced their strongest sides, with Burnley wing half Billy Watson making his 100th consecutive appearance for the club.

Despite the importance of the occasion, the tie was played in great spirit which was reflected by the mood of a good-natured crowd. The defining moment of the game came midway through the first half when Tommy Boyle came up for a corner that was delivered perfectly from the right by winger Eddie Mosscrop. The slightly built centre half belied his lack of inches to climb above the defence and head the ball past 'keeper Alf Robinson. Having gained the lead, the visitors successfully adopted defensive tactics to cling on to their

Skipper Tommy Boyle leaps to head home the winner.

slim advantage for the remainder of the match. With the benefit of the wind after the interval, the Rovers' attack, with big-money signings Jock Simpson and Danny Shea, threw everything at Burnley in an attempt to snatch an equaliser. They were denied by a defence superbly marshalled by Boyle, in which 'keeper Jerry Dawson was outstanding. The *Daily News & Leader* reported: 'One felt a tinge of sorrow for Crompton. He had fought a magnificent battle assisted by plucky and clever colleagues, but they had met eleven most determined opponents who got the one goal of a game in which they were inferior in attack but supreme in defence. The brilliant spoiling movements of Boyle and his colleagues undoubtedly earned Burnley the right to appear in the semi-final for the first time in the club's history.'

Burnley's own cup dreams were ended in the semi-final by eventual League Champions Sunderland. After a goalless draw, the Wearsiders won the replay by the odd goal in five, before failing in the quest for the double, losing to Aston Villa in the final. Burnley had the consolation of gaining promotion and the following season succeeded in winning the FA Cup. As for Bob Crompton, it was said that he was inconsolable after the disappointing exit from the competition against Burnley, but a Rovers supporter took the result more philosophically:

BLACKBURN ROVERS' FAREWELL TO THE CUP

Well beaten upon our own ground,
No longer a dream we pursue;
O happiness not to be found,
Unattainable treasure adieu!

We looked upon you as our spoil,
We thought we were really hot stuff;
But Burnley were right on the 'Boyle',
And so we weren't half hot enough.

We're sorry you've bid us begone,
But we're not going to cry, to be sure;
For the odds are quite 10 to 1 on,
We shall see you ere long at Turf Moor.

J.W. Briggs

Blackburn Rovers (2-3-5)

Alf Robinson; Bob Crompton, Arthur Cowell; Albert Walmsley, Percy Smith, Billy Bradshaw; Jock Simpson, Danny Shea, Wattie Aitkenhead, Eddie Latherton, Walter Anthony. Manager: Robert Middleton.

Burnley (2-3-5)

Jerry Dawson; Tom Bamford, David Taylor; Bill McLaren, Tommy Boyle, Billy Watson; Eddie Mosscrop, Dick Lindley, Bert Freeman, Ted Hodgson, William Husband. Manager: John Haworth.

FA CUP SIXTH ROUND   8 MARCH 1952
BLACKBURN ROVERS 3   BURNLEY 1
Attendance: 52,920

Blackburn Rovers enhanced their reputation as bonny cup fighters with a spirited second-half comeback which overwhelmed their neighbours and took the club into the FA Cup semi-final for the fourteenth time in their history. A classic cup encounter brought together two teams a division apart, although home advantage balanced the odds for Second Division Blackburn Rovers who had already proved their ability to beat First Division opposition, eliminating West Bromwich Albion in the previous round. Burnley threatened to pose stiffer opposition, having disposed of 1950 cup finalists Liverpool in the fifth round. After a nervy start to the derby by both sides, the Clarets dominated the first half. Playing neat, flowing football, the Clarets took a thoroughly deserved lead after half an hour. England international Billy Elliott had proved particularly dangerous on the right flank until he was cut down in a foul challenge by his marker Ron Suart. While the badly shaken winger was off the field receiving treatment, Jimmy Adamson floated the free-kick in from the right and the ball ran loose to Les Shannon who pulled the ball back for Jackie Chew to hit the opener. Billy Elliott returned to the fray but was immediately floored again and his injuries forced him to switch places with Bill Holden and play at centre forward where he hobbled throughout the remainder of the game. The effectiveness of the Burnley attack was undermined and suddenly the balance of the match had swung in Blackburn's favour. As half-time approached, the visitors clung on to their advantage and survived a series of corner kicks before Rovers levelled in injury time. Winger Alec Glover fired in a fierce shot which was deflected off a defender into the path of inside left Albert Nightingale who made no mistake, beating 'keeper Jimmy Strong from close range. Rovers took the field with renewed confidence after the interval and quickly took a grip on proceedings. They went in front after fifty-eight minutes when centre forward Bill Holmes flashed in a header to convert Nightingale's cross. With eight minutes remaining, Rovers made certain of the game through the tenacity of Holmes. The England amateur international seemed to be chasing a lost cause when he ran half the length of the field in pursuit of a long clearance. The perseverance of Rovers' danger-man paid off when he beat Jock Aird and Tommy Cummings in a tussle for the ball and squared it for Glover to collect his second goal of the match. Burnley strove hard to get back into the game and went near in the closing moments when a drive by Bill Holden struck the bar – but the visitors finished the game a well-beaten side.

Blackburn Rovers had won the FA Cup a record six times and hopes ran high among the Ewood Park faithful that the club could add to this total. Harry Healess had been the last Rovers skipper to lift the trophy in 1928 and it seemed a good omen that the present cup run had coincided with his return

Summary of the cup derby through the eyes of cartoonist 'Tipping'.

to the club as senior coach. Sadly, the team's luck ran out when they were drawn to face cup-holders Newcastle United in the semi-final. After a goalless draw at Hillsborough, the Magpies won a hard-fought replay at Elland Road, going on to retain the trophy by beating Arsenal at Wembley.

Blackburn Rovers (2-3-5)

Reg Elvy; Ron Suart, Bill Eckersley; Jackie Campbell, Willie Kelly, Ron Clayton; Jackie Wharton, Eddie Crossan, Bill Holmes, Albert Nightingale, Alec Glover.
Manager: Jackie Bestall.

Burnley (2-3-5)

Jimmy Strong; Jock Aird, Harold Mather; Jimmy Adamson, Tommy Cummings, Reg Attwell; Jackie Chew, Bill Morris, Bill Holden, Les Shannon, Billy Elliott.
Manager: Frank Hill.

FA CUP FOURTH ROUND   28 JANUARY 1959
BLACKBURN ROVERS 1   BURNLEY 2
Attendance: 43,752

The first attempt to play this cup tie ended in farce and severely tested the patience of 44,300 East Lancashire supporters who parted with their hard-earned money to see a seasonal pantomime on ice. Ewood Park was coated in packed snow which the referee thought would thaw under the bright winter sunshine. However, freezing divots made the conditions dangerous and after the players had risked serious injury slipping and sliding around the pitch, the scoreless match was abandoned at half-time. This decision did not go down well with columnist 'Man on the Terraces' who voiced his displeasure in the *Lancashire Evening Telegraph*: 'I should be called "Mug on the Terraces", today I pay my two shillings and expect to see 90 minutes play.' Nevertheless, four days later, another huge crowd turned up to witness the outcome of this cup clash. A marginally improved ground covered in sand drew this amusing observation from local sports correspondent 'Centurion': 'The pitch looked as though a high wind had blown a top dust off the Sahara Desert to the Siberian steppes.' In such dire conditions, Rovers surprisingly recalled Bryan Douglas after a two-month injury lay-off.

In a thrilling encounter, the home side took control in the opening stages and took the lead in the sixth minute when Peter Dobing converted a pass from centre forward Tommy Johnson. Just before half-time, Burnley squandered a golden opportunity to draw level when striker Jimmy Robson struck the crossbar and winger Brian Pilkington sliced the rebound wide with the goal at his mercy. Rovers were unlucky not to extend their lead shortly after the break when Roy Vernon hit the net with a terrific twenty-five-yard drive. The home fans were incensed when the referee spotted Bryan Douglas wide on the right in an offside position and disallowed the goal – although it did not seem possible that the winger could be adjudged to be interfering with play. Burnley rode their luck and, on the hour, grabbed an equaliser through Jimmy McIlroy, who unleashed a shot into a crowded penalty area which evaded unsighted 'keeper Harry Leyland. Blackburn stormed back and a Dobing piledriver brought a world-class save out of England 'keeper Colin McDonald. The visitors' assurance in the worsening conditions underfoot, and the willingness of their half-backs Seith, Miller and Adamson to tackle wholeheartedly on a treacherous pitch, eventually turned the balance of the match. The Clarets were clearly the better side in the closing stages and only faultless handling by Leyland, allied with sterling defensive work by centre half Matt Woods and skipper Ron Clayton kept them at bay. As supporters were contemplating the prospect of paying out another entrance fee for a replay at Turf Moor, another controversial decision sensationally brought about a result. Two minutes from time, full-back Bill Eckersley turned the ball back to his 'keeper and an

Blackburn 'keeper Harry Leyland bravely foils Jimmy Robson on an ice-bound pitch in the first encounter which was abandoned at half-time.

eagle-eyed linesman ruled that the ball had marginally crossed the byline before Harry Leyland scooped it up. A corner was given and Burnley's outstanding forward Jimmy Robson flashed home a superb header from John Connelly's inch-perfect cross. Moments later, Robson ran through the defence and netted again, but this time the effort was disallowed for offside before the final whistle sounded and the jubilant Clarets were through to the fifth round.

Magnanimous in defeat, Blackburn manager Dally Duncan was the first to admit that the better team had won and wished the victors well. Five weeks later, his team gained their revenge over Burnley with a 4-1 League win at Ewood Park in what proved to be a bad week for their derby rivals. Four days earlier, the Clarets' promising cup run had been ended in a sixth-round replay at Aston Villa.

Blackburn Rovers (2-3-5)
Harry Leyland; Ken Taylor, Bill Eckersley; Ron Clayton, Matt Woods, Mick McGrath; Bryan Douglas, Peter Dobing, Tommy Johnson, Roy Stephenson, Ally MacLeod. Manager: Dally Duncan.

Burnley (2-3-5)
Colin McDonald; Tommy Cummings, David Smith; Bobby Seith, Brian Miller, Jimmy Adamson; John Connelly, Jimmy McIlroy, Ray Pointer, Jimmy Robson, Brian Pilkington. Manager: Harry Potts.

FA CUP SIXTH ROUND   12 MARCH 1960

BURNLEY 3   BLACKBURN ROVERS 3

Attendance: 51,501

East Lancashire supporters lucky enough to have obtained a ticket gathered at Turf Moor to witness one of the most incredible matches in the history of the fixture. Both sides had their sights set on Wembley after reaching the quarter-finals the hard way. In each of the three previous rounds, Burnley had been drawn away to clubs in lower divisions and needed a replay to overcome Lincoln, Bradford and Swansea, while Blackburn had also won replays against Sunderland and Blackpool before pulling off a stunning victory over Spurs at White Hart Lane. A week before the cup clash, Burnley had beaten Rovers at home by a single goal in a League match and were slight favourites to go through to the semi-finals.

The first half was a dour affair and gave no indication of the thrills to come. Cup nerves seemed to affect the teams and both defences were on top in the early exchanges. As the game progressed, Rovers enjoyed territorial advantage and seemed most likely to break the deadlock, but when tested, Burnley 'keeper Adam Blacklaw proved equal to the task, cutting out dangerous crosses and producing some smart saves. The match was transformed shortly after the interval through the genius of midfield maestro Jimmy McIlroy. In a fifteen-minute spell, he tormented the Rovers defence and the visitors suddenly found themselves three goals down. For the opening goal, the Northern Ireland international found Brian Pilkington with a cross-field pass which the left-winger took in his stride and hit a terrific right-foot shot which beat Harry Leyland's despairing dive and dipped beneath the angle of the crossbar at the far post. Minutes later, McIlroy gathered the ball near the right corner flag and jinked his way along the byline past three defenders before slipping the ball to Ray Pointer who turned the ball in at the near post. Rovers were left reeling when winger John Connelly latched onto skipper Jimmy Adamson's long pass inside the full-back, before skipping inside the penalty area and chipping the ball cleverly over the advancing Leyland. The result appeared a foregone conclusion and Burnley fans now firmly believed that the club's name was on the trophy. With seventeen minutes remaining, the hopes of travelling supporters were rekindled when a harmless-looking shot from Peter Dobing bounced awkwardly and struck full-back Alex Elder on the arm and the referee gave a penalty. It seemed an extremely harsh decision, but as Bryan Douglas stroked home the spot kick it should have been no more than a consolation goal for Rovers. However, three minutes later, Dobing fired in another speculative shot from twenty-five yards which somehow evaded the unsighted Blacklaw. Their advantage now reduced to one goal, confidence visibly drained from the Clarets and Rovers skipper Ronnie Clayton drove his side forward in search of an equaliser. Four minutes from the end it came via a free-kick taken

Mick McGrath (beyond defenders Angus and Adamson) scores the dramatic equaliser as Ally McLeod closes in at the near post.

by centre half Matt Woods. The ball was half-cleared to Clayton whose shot from the edge of the box flew into a mass of bodies and fell into the path of Mick McGrath who stabbed at the ball from close range. Burnley defenders watched in horror as the ball crept into the net off the inside of the upright. Blackburn suddenly looked capable of winning the tie and the closing moments were agony for the home supporters who breathed a sigh of relief when the referee blew the final whistle. The official was booed from the field for a poor penalty decision that had seemingly robbed Burnley of victory. Nevertheless, Rovers' fighting spirit and three scrappy goals had matched the brilliant efforts of their skilful opponents. Furthermore, they had dealt a severe psychological blow to a Burnley team who thought they had the match won and now had only four days to recover from the shock before facing the replay at Ewood Park.

Burnley (2-3-5)
Adam Blacklaw; John Angus, Alex Elder; Bobby Seith, Brian Miller, Jimmy Adamson; John Connelly, Jimmy McIlroy, Ray Pointer, Jimmy Robson, Brian Pilkington. Manager: Harry Potts.

Blackburn Rovers (2-3-5)
Harry Leyland; John Bray, Dave Whelan; Ron Clayton, Matt Woods, Mick McGrath; Louis Bimpson, Peter Dobing, Derek Dougan, Bryan Douglas, Ally MacLeod. Manager: Dally Duncan.

FA CUP SIXTH ROUND   16 MARCH 1960
(REPLAY)

BLACKBURN ROVERS 2   BURNLEY 0 (AFTER EXTRA TIME)

Attendance: 53,839

With a semi-final date at Maine Road against Sheffield Wednesday awaiting the winners, East Lancashire fans assembled at Ewood Park for a nerve-tingling replay which went to extra time before the outcome was decided. Burnley had tried to shrug off the disappointment of throwing away a three-goal lead at Turf Moor by preparing at Blackpool and both sides announced unchanged teams. A repeat of the previous Saturday's six-goal thriller at Turf Moor was too much to expect and both defences were a good deal tighter for this evening match. Rovers always carried the greater threat and pressed continuously without creating many clear-cut chances. The only incident of note during the first half concerned two Northern Ireland international colleagues, Rovers' colourful Derek 'Cheyenne' Dougan and Burnley's midfield architect Jimmy McIlroy. 'Mac' had an uncharacteristic off-day and incensed the home crowd when a clumsy challenge felled the centre forward who left the field for treatment just before half-time. During the interval, the press box were informed that Dougan was fit to resume, but there was concern on the terraces when Rovers took the field with ten men. As the teams lined up for the restart, cynical reporters observed the 'Doog' make a dramatic entrance by shuffling back into the arena to the cheers of the relieved Blackburn supporters. Rovers stayed on top in a scrappy second period and Burnley were under constant pressure before they broke away to create their only real chance of the night just before the end of ninety minutes. Winger John Connelly hit a fine left-foot shot which was brilliantly turned around the post by 'keeper Harry Leyland, who up to that point had enjoyed a quiet evening between the posts. As thoughts turned to the possibility of a second replay, Rovers broke the deadlock in the thirteenth minute of extra time when full-back John Angus was penalised for a foul on Ally MacLeod. Rovers' best forward Bryan Douglas floated across the free-kick and Dougan out-jumped marker Brian Miller to head the ball down into the path of Peter Dobing who ran onto the ball and smashed a low shot past 'keeper Adam Blacklaw which went in off the inside of a post. Rovers' supporters surged onto the field and when the pitch was cleared, there was a further delay before the ball was recovered from a souvenir hunter who had caught the ball when the 'Doog' had taken it from the net and belted it onto the terraces. Burnley pushed defenders up in a desperate attempt to snatch an equaliser but with a minute to go, fell further behind when Ally MacLeod got on the end of Louis Bimpson's flick from Ronnie Clayton's long throw to loop a header into the roof of the net.

The crestfallen Clarets realised they were out of the cup, but would later have the admirable consolation of climbing to the top of the First Division in the very

From left to right: Burnley forwards Ray Pointer, John Connelly and Brian Pilkington 'warm up' for the replay during training at Blackpool.

last game of the season. Rovers had denied their derby rivals the chance of achieving the League and cup 'double', and having reached their third semi-final in eight years, cleared the last hurdle to book a place in the final against a Wolverhampton Wanderers team still smarting from being pipped to the League title by Burnley. The blue and whites' big day ended in disaster when Dave Whelan became the latest victim of the 'Wembley Hoodoo'. The unfortunate full-back was stretchered off in the first half as ten-man Rovers went down 3-0. The seasonal showpiece was ruined as a spectacle and brought renewed calls for the introduction of substitutes. A minority of Blackburn supporters spoiled the occasion by venting their frustration at the Wolves players who were pelted with rubbish at the end of a match which was thereafter remembered as 'The Dustbin Final'.

Blackburn Rovers (2-3-5)

Harry Leyland; John Bray, Dave Whelan; Ron Clayton, Matt Woods, Mick McGrath; Louis Bimpson, Peter Dobing, Derek Dougan, Bryan Douglas, Ally MacLeod. Manager: Dally Duncan.

Burnley (2-3-5)

Adam Blacklaw; John Angus, Alex Elder; Bobby Seith, Brian Miller, Jimmy Adamson; John Connelly, Jimmy McIlroy, Ray Pointer, Jimmy Robson, Brian Pilkington. Manager: Harry Potts.

ANGLO-SCOTTISH CUP (PRELIMINARY GROUP)	12 AUGUST 1978
BLACKBURN ROVERS 1	BURNLEY 1
Attendance: 9,791	

As Blackburn Rovers and Burnley had both previously beaten Preston and Blackpool in the pre-season competition, this cup derby was in effect, the Anglo-Scottish North-West group decider, with the winners assured of going through to meet Scottish opposition in the quarter-finals. The Clarets had amassed a superior goal tally in their two group matches and therefore required only a draw to bypass their Second Division East Lancashire rivals.

The match got off to a sensational start when Burnley winger Tony Morley, brought in as a late replacement for injured Northern Irish international Terry Cochrane, created a goal out of nothing in the third minute. Collecting a clearance in his own half, the winger raced seventy yards down the touchline, beating marker John Bailey twice in the process, then swung over a cross which took a deflection off a defender before reaching Malcolm Smith who could not fail to score standing only five yards out. In a ding-dong opening, chances went begging at both ends before Rovers levelled after only nine minutes. First-team debut boy Simon Garner built up the move on the left in an interchange of passes with John Bailey whose cross was met ten yards out by the lunge of Noel Brotherston, who was at full stretch as he poked a shot just wide of 'keeper Alan Stevenson's left hand. The crowd were prepared for a goal feast, but were to be disappointed as the match went slowly off the boil. With Tony Morley's blistering pace and Peter Noble's impressive form, Burnley remained on top throughout the first period but were always susceptible to a counterattack with the home side looking sharp on the break.

The second half began quietly until the tempo suddenly picked up with the best move of the match. John Bailey and Stuart Metcalfe combined to rip open the Burnley defence only to be let down by Garner's weak shot over the top. Blackburn were also thwarted by some desperate defending when a goal-bound shot from Noel Brotherston was deflected wide, Martin Fowler was floored by a last-ditch tackle and a blistering drive from midfield dynamo Stuart Metcalfe was saved at full stretch by Stevenson. As the match drew to a conclusion, futher clear-cut chances to clinch the game were squandered by the home side; Glenn Keeley had a golden opportunity but headed well wide of an open goal, then Alan Stevenson denied Simon Garner with a diving save. Rovers piled on the pressure and were unlucky when a three-man passing movement involving Garner, Aston and Bailey ended with Garner shooting just wide of the angle of the post and the crossbar. In the last minute, Tony Morley almost provided a shock finish to match his opening burst when he narrowly failed to convert a cross from fellow winger Steve Kindon.

Burnley skipper Peter Noble holds the Anglo-Scottish trophy aloft.

Burnley's prize for this victory was a tie against Scottish giants Celtic who were surprisingly beaten in both legs of a memorable quarter-final by an aggregate score of 3-1. Following this fantastic result, the Clarets almost stumbled in the semis against Third Division Mansfield. The second leg went to extra time before Burnley clinched a place in the final after a nerve-jangling penalty shoot-out went 8-7 in their favour. Their final opponents were Oldham who were resoundingly beaten 4-1 in the first leg at Boundary Park and although the Latics won the return 1-0, the trophy was presented to Clarets' triumphant skipper Peter Noble before a modest crowd of 10,000 at Turf Moor.

Blackburn (4-3-3)

John Butcher; Kevin Hird, Glenn Keeley, John Waddington, John Bailey; Stuart Metcalfe, Martin Fowler, Tony Parkes; Noel Brotherston, Simon Garner, John Aston. Subs: Neil Ramsbottom, John Curtis. Manager: Jim Iley.

Burnley (4-3-3)

Alan Stevenson; Derek Scott, Jim Thompson, Billy Rodaway, Ian Brenann; Peter Noble, Billy Ingham, Malcolm Smith; Tony Morley, Paul Fletcher, Steve Kindon. Subs: Brian Hall, Bill O'Rourke. Manager: Harry Potts.

LANCASHIRE MANX CUP FINAL   13 AUGUST 1985
BLACKBURN ROVERS 1   BURNLEY 0
Attendance: 6,017

In 1982, the magnificent old Lancashire Senior Cup trophy had been dusted off for presentation to the winners of this pre-season tournament sponsored by the Isle of Man Tourist Board. For the fourth consecutive season, Blackburn Rovers had made it to the final, while Burnley were making their first appearance at this stage of the competition. The prospect of the East Lancashire rivals meeting in the final had come about when the blue and whites had emerged from their group matches against Wigan, Blackpool and Preston to face the Clarets who had eased their way past opposition from Bury, Rochdale and Bolton to set up this highly entertaining cup derby played at Ewood Park.

The performance of the visitors in the first half belied the fact that they were now languishing in the Fourth Division having been relegated to the basement League for the first time in their history the previous season. The Clarets completely outplayed their Second Division opponents and created enough chances to settle the match but were let down by lacklustre finishing. Rovers old boy Kevin Hird seemed eager to prove a point against his former club and fired in a fierce shot which brought the best out of Rovers' custodian Terry Gennoe. He then set up a clear-cut opportunity for Steve Taylor with a telling pass which put the centre forward right through the defence, but the chance went begging when he somehow contrived to hit his shot straight at the 'keeper. Fellow striker Wayne Biggins also missed a golden opportunity to put his side ahead when he lost his marker to meet a cross before thudding a header well wide of the target. Rovers were on the ropes and may have been showing signs of fatigue as this was their eighth game in sixteen days, but whatever the reason, manager Bob Saxton must have been a relieved man when the whistle sounded for half-time and his players trooped off to the dressing room extremely fortunate to be still on level terms with their goal intact.

Having survived the onslaught of the first period, Rovers came out after the interval fired up by a pep talk and soon had their opponents on the back foot. In a stunning reversal of fortune, only Clarets 'keeper Joe Neenan kept a rampant attack at bay with a string of brilliant saves in an inspired second-half performance which deserved to take the match into extra time. Time and again he provided an obstinate last line of defence until Rovers finally found a way past him with twelve minutes to go. Fittingly, the game was eventually decided by a superb piece of individualism by Simon Garner. The striker received a received a pass from Jimmy Quinn and showed he had only one thing on his mind as he cut inside full-back Geoff Palmer and bore down purposefully on the Burnley goal. This time Joe Keenan had no chance as the talented striker

Simon Garner's strike secured
the cup for Blackburn.

unleashed a powerful shot into the roof of the net which left the flying 'keeper desperately clawing at thin air. Burnley gamely tried to fight their way back into the match and pressed for an equaliser but were made to regret their early catalogue of misses in front of goal as the Blackburn team finished strongly and celebrated at the final whistle by picking up the Lancashire Manx trophy for the second time. Burnley supporters left Ewood Park feeling aggrieved that their team's first-half performance had come to naught, but in common with all terrace philosophers, they doubtless recognised the wisdom of the old soccer adage, 'Football is a game of two halves!'

Blackburn (4-3-3)
Terry Gennoe; David Hamilton, Glenn Keeley, David Mail, Mick Rathbone; Simon Barker, John Lowey, Noel Brotherston; Ian Miller, Jimmy Quinn, Simon Garner. Manager: Bob Saxton.

Burnley (4-3-3)
Joe Neenan; Geoff Palmer, Jim Heggarty, Ray Deakin, Peter Hampton; Kevin Hird, Vince Overson, Phil Malley; Nigel Grewcock, Steve Taylor, Wayne Biggins. Manager: Martin Buchan.

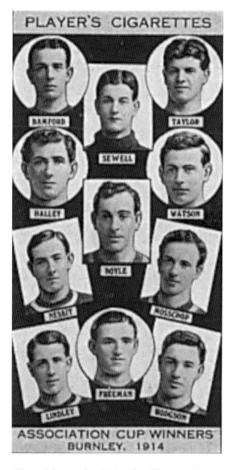

Above left: Burnley 1914. The Clarets' only cup success came in the last final played at the Kennington Oval and the first to be attended by a reigning monarch – King George V. Since that triumph Burnley have reached two more finals, finishing as runners-up in 1947 and 1962.

Above right: Blackburn 1928. This was the only FA Cup success of the twentieth century for Rovers who had previously won the trophy in 1884, 1885, 1886, 1890 and 1891. They had finished as runners-up in their first final in 1882 and were also beaten finalists in 1960.

3

DERBY DOUBLES

Burnley, East Lancashire Charity Cup winners 1893. Centre forward Peter Turnbull (seated at the front alongside the trophy) became the first member of a exclusive club to appear in a Football League match for Burnley and Blackburn Rovers. The list of players signed by the East Lancashire rivals forms an impressive fantasy squad.

Edgar Chadwick
Midfield
Born: Blackburn, 1870

Local boy Edgar Chadwick was a player of prodigious talent. Making his debut for Rovers in 1887, during the last season of friendly matches before the Football League was founded, the seventeen-year-old formed a lethal strike force with Jack Southworth, scoring three goals in four FA Cup matches. He reluctantly left Ewood Park when his father persuaded him that he could obtain better financial rewards with Everton.

Moving to Merseyside for eleven years, Edgar made 300 appearances and scored 110 goals, collecting a Football League Championship medal in 1891 and a FA Cup finalists' medal in 1897. By now he had became one of the country's best-known players, winning 7 England caps. Arriving at Turf Moor in 1899, he was the club's top scorer, but his influence failed to save Burnley from relegation. After one season he moved on to Liverpool, then to Southampton, who won the Southern League Championship in 1901 and the following season reached the FA Cup final in a side which included England cricket and soccer international C.B. Fry.

When his playing days in non-League soccer ended in 1908, Edgar became a soccer missionary, becoming the first English coach to work abroad in Holland and Germany before the advent of war curtailed this activity. Thereafter he returned to Lancashire and came out of retirement to play for Blackburn in wartime games while pursuing a trade as a baker in his home town.

Tom Nicol
Full-Back/Forward
Born: Linlithgow, 1870

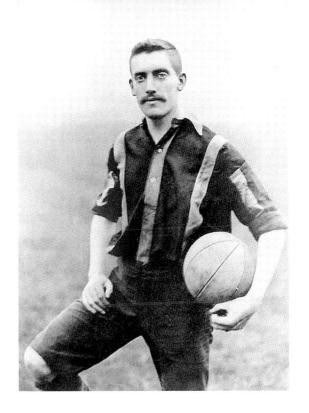

Centre forward Tom Nicol became a goalscoring sensation when he notched a hat-trick on his League debut in March 1891. He remains the only player in Burnley's history to achieve this feat. In addition, the opponents on the receiving end of a 6-2 thrashing were the reigning League Champions Preston North End, whom Burnley had never beaten before. Yet despite this auspicious start and no serious rivals to lead the attack during his five years at the club, it remains a mystery why Burnley seemed reluctant to persevere with him in this position. Signed from Scottish club Mossend Swifts, Tom alternated between centre forward and the right wing during his first full season and cracked in 18 goals in 27 cup and League matches. He then proved to be even more versatile turning out regularly for the club at full-back and centre half. In April 1896, he was selected on the wing for the last game of the season, a home derby against Blackburn Rovers, and collected his third hat-trick for the club (see match report, pages 12-13). Despite losing 6-0, Rovers obviously took note, because the following season Tom was on his way to Ewood Park. However, after 19 games being utilised at left-back, right wing and centre forward he moved on at the end of the season to Southampton where he later linked up with former Blackburn and Burnley forward Edgar Chadwick when the Saints won the Southern League Championship in 1901.

Albert Walmsley

Defender
Born: Blackburn,
  21 October 1885

The Football League came under attack for continuing after the outbreak of the First World War. The sight of healthy young men making a living from sport while many of their generation were dying on the battlefields of Europe was too much to bear for many critics. As a result normal soccer was suspended in the summer of 1915 and Blackburn Rovers decided not to enter the regional tournaments the following season. Consequently many Rovers players gave their services to other clubs. Bob Crompton, George Chapman, Joe Hodkinson and Eddie Latherton (soon to make the supreme sacrifice for his country) turned out for Blackpool, while Albert Cowell, Johny Orr and Albert Walmsley joined Burnley. Industrious, hard-tackling wing half Albert Walmsley made the biggest impact at Turf Moor, making 21 appearances for the Clarets before Ewood Park reopened for business in 1916. At Burnley, he took over from George Halley playing alongside his legendary colleagues, Tommy Boyle and Billy Watson in a team that included many members of the 1914 FA Cup-winning side. A vital cog in Blackburn's League Championship sides of 1911 and 1913, the First World War effectively ended Albert's League career and after one post-war season he left Ewood Park having made 335 appearances for his hometown club whom he had served since 1902.

Ron Sewell
Goalkeeper
Born: Wingate, 19 July 1890

Burnley were so impressed with their 1913 FA Cup opponents Gainsborough Trinity they bought the whole defence! Among them was goalkeeper Ronnie Sewell who had the unenviable task of deputising for the incomparable Jerry Dawson, who still holds the appearance record for Burnley. Opportunities for first-team experience were rare but Ronnie got an unexpected chance to shine when Dawson was injured in the drawn 1914 FA Cup semi-final against Sheffield United. Completely unfazed, the understudy stepped out of the wings for the replay and kept a clean sheet as a goal from skipper Tommy Boyle took the Clarets through to the final. In a nerve-wracking sequel for club and supporters, a magnanimous Dawson pronounced himself unfit for the final and Sewell received a winners medal by holding the Liverpool attack at bay in another single-goal victory settled by a Bert Freeman strike.

Like many players, Ronnie's progress was interrupted by the First World War and in 1920 he moved to Blackburn where he proved his class over the next seven seasons. His form was a revelation and could not be overlooked by the England selectors. In 1924, at the age of thirty-three, he won a well-deserved cap against Wales in a full international which was played at Ewood Park. Sadly, his career was ended by a broken leg in 1926. He attempted a comeback but was forced to call it a day a year later. The injury cost him the chance of a glorious swansong the following season when Rovers won the 1928 FA Cup. On this occasion it was Jock Crawford who benefitted from another goalkeeper's misfortune.

Levy Thorpe
Central Defender/Midfield
Born: Seaham Harbour,
   18 November 1889

The legendary Burnley half-back line of Halley, Boyle and Watson, which flourished either side of the First World War, has long overshadowed the contribution of Levy Thorpe who was most unfortunate to miss out on club and representative honours. Signed from Blackpool in October 1913, Levy deputised for all three of the great men in Burnley's League matches, but took no part in the side which successfully lifted the FA Cup for the only time in the club's history. The following season, George Halley was displaced by Thorpe as Burnley climbed to fourth in the First Division during the last campaign before League Football was suspended for the duration of the First World War.

   Illness once forced Levy to withdraw from the Football League team and he was selected only as reserve for an England Victory international in 1919. That season George Halley found himself converted to left-back as Thorpe occupied the right half berth for twenty games until a double deal resulted in the transfer of himself and goalkeeper Ronnie Sewell to Blackburn Rovers in February 1920. This move meant that the stylish half-back missed out again the following season, when Burnley carried off the League Championship, while Thorpe was an ever-present in the Rovers side which finished in mid-table. Now at the veteran stage, Levy served Rovers for three seasons before his place in the side came under threat from future international Harry Healess. Surplus to requirements, Levy moved to Lincoln City and then Rochdale where he ended his League career.

Sam Wadsworth
Full-Back
Born: Darwen,
   13 September 1896

On Blackburn Rovers' books as an amateur at the outbreak of the First World War, Sam Wadsworth must rank as one the best players to be overlooked by the club. With wartime service limiting his availability, he turned out sporadically, making seven appearances in wartime League matches, usually selected at inside left or left wing. With no offer forthcoming from Rovers after hostilities had ceased, Sam turned professional with non-League Nelson, near Burnley. His performances soon came to the notice of legendary Huddersfield Town manager Herbert Chapman, who snapped him up from under the noses of the East Lancashire League clubs in March 1921. Sam was converted to left-back and for the next seven seasons was a regular in the great side that won three consecutive League Championships between 1923 and 1926. Making 312 appearances for the Terriers, Sam represented the Football League and was awarded 9 full caps, making his debut in the same England team as Burnley greats Jerry Dawson and Bob Kelly. He also lined up in Huddersfield's FA cup-winning team of 1922 but was disappointed to be omitted from the final side which was beaten by his old club Blackburn Rovers in 1928. A year later he moved to Turf Moor where he made only seven first-team appearances for the Clarets in two seasons before taking up a coaching post and settling in Holland. Despite making his reputation elsewhere, Sam remains one of the most distinguished players to have worn the colours of both East Lancashire clubs.

Jack Bruton

Winger
Born: Westhoughton,
21 November 1903

Attracting the attention of many club scouts while playing for Horwich RMI in 1925, it was Burnley who made a decisive move for miner Jack Bruton and it took little persuasion for him to sign professional forms on an upturned tub at the pit head. It proved an inspired signing as the speedy winger came straight into the side and scored on his debut. At Turf Moor he won 3 England caps before Blackburn Rovers paid a club-record fee of £6,500 for his services in December 1929. During ten years at Ewood Park, Jack made over 300 appearances, but played only once in the club's Second Division Championship campaign before the Football League was suspended at the outset of the Second World War. He turned out in wartime games before announcing his retirement in 1943.

Jack continued to serve the club in a backroom capacity as assistant trainer, then assistant manager, before taking over as manager in 1947 when Will Scott retired through ill health. His appointment could not save Rovers from relegation and when the club failed to challenge for promotion the following season he was relieved of duty. In 1950 he became manager of Bournemouth and remained with them for six years. Settling on the South Coast, he stayed in touch with the game by scouting for various clubs including Blackburn. He remains the only player to have scored for both clubs in East Lancashire derbies and is the ideal candidate to lead the fantasy squad (see pages 71-72).

Peter O'Dowd
Central Defender
Born: Halifax,
   26 February 1908

Yorkshireman Peter O'Dowd broke the mould of the purely defensive 'stopper' employed to combat changes in the offside law and was a footballing centre half exceptionally comfortable on the ball. This style was not always fully appreciated during his first three seasons of League football at Ewood Park where he was usually preferred at wing half. In March 1930 he was transferred to Burnley who were struggling near the foot of the First Division. In his second game he scored the winner against his former club in a five-goal derby at Turf Moor but the result did not save his team from relegation (see match report, pages 82-83). An ever-present in the side the following season, he was selected for an FA tour of Canada where his performances enhanced his international prospects. Cash-strapped Burnley could not turn down an offer of £5,000 from Chelsea. Peter's debut for the Pensioners in November 1931 was less than promising as his new team were thrashed 7-2 by Everton with Dixie Dean scoring five, but four months later he won the first of 3 England caps. With teammate Alex Cheyne he became one of the first British players attracted by lucrative deals abroad when he signed for the French club Valenciennes in September 1935. Unfortunately, they found that the grass was not greener across the Channel. Disillusioned, Peter returned to England eighteen months later and tried to resurrect his career with Torquay United. The Devon club paid a club-record fee for his services but after only 7 appearances a broken leg brought his playing days to a sad end at the age of twenty-nine.

Arthur Cunliffe
Winger
Born: Blackrod, Wigan
   5 February 1909

A lightning-quick winger with superb close control and crossing skills allied to an eye for goal, Arthur Cunliffe was discovered while playing for Chorley and arrived at Ewood Park in January 1928. The eighteen-year-old youngster was consigned to learn his trade in the reserves while the first-team trod the road to Wembley and FA Cup success. Originally a right-winger Arthur effortlessly switched to the opposite flank for his League debut in 1930. This was to accommodate a new signing from Burnley on the other wing – Jack Bruton – although Arthur would emulate him by gaining international honours and playing for both East Lancashire clubs. When inside forward Ronnie Dix was signed from Bristol Rovers in May 1932, he forged an impressive left-wing partnership with Arthur, whose brilliance at the start of the next campaign attracted the attention of the selectors and he was awarded 2 England caps. To the astonishment of supporters, both players were transferred at the end of the season to Aston Villa, who had just finished runners-up in the old First Division. The highlight of Arthur's eighteen-month stay at Villa Park was reaching the FA Cup semi-final in 1934 before the team lost to eventual winners Manchester City. A spell at Middlesbrough was followed by a move to Turf Moor in April 1937 but Arthur failed to recapture the form of old and after a handful of games he was sold to Hull City.

Jack Chew
Winger
Born: Blackburn,
    13 May 1920

Local boy Jackie Chew was on the books of Blackburn Rovers as an amateur but his career did not take off until war was declared and regional Leagues set up following the suspension of the Football League. The sharp-shooting winger made 23 appearances in two seasons for Rovers before answering his country's call and serving in the RAF. In 1945, he turned out as a 'guest' for Leeds United and Burnley. Accepting professional terms with the Clarets, honours came immediately as he played a full part in the club's post-war success. The Clarets enjoyed a great season, gaining promotion from the Second Division and reaching the 1947 FA Cup final. Back in the First Division, Jackie's ability to cut in and shoot powerfully from the flank enabled him to become the club's leading marksman with eleven goals in 1949. The bandy-legged footballer, known affectionately as 'Cowboy' by the fans, often came in for some good-natured stick in derbies played at Ewood Park, particularly when he scored the opener against his hometown club in a 1952 FA Cup tie (see match report, pages 40-41). In 1954, at the age of thirty-four, Jackie moved on to end his playing days with Bradford City, having scored 41 goals in 248 appearances for Burnley. However, he was seen in action for many seasons more at Turf Moor – turning out on the adjoining cricket field. A talented middle-order batsman, he captained Rishton in the Lancashire League and for many summers renewed his acquaintance with former Claret and Wembley wing partner Peter Kippax who welcomed him as skipper of Burnley CC.

Roy Stephenson
Midfield/Winger
Born: Cook, 27 May 1932

Joining Burnley in 1950, Roy Stephenson found it difficult to hold down a regular first-team spot during his six years at Turf Moor, where he could be relied upon to perform consistently when called on to fill a variety of forward positions. In 1955, an extended run in the side at inside forward earned him a trial for England Under 23s, but he failed to win final selection. A year later, his career seemed to be in decline when he moved to Second Division Rotherham, but Burnley fans had not heard the last of this determined character. His form at Rotherham attracted the attention of Blackburn manager Johnny Carey and Roy became a member of the squad which won promotion from the Second Division in 1958. He also played in every round of Rovers' run to the FA Cup semi-final before they lost to eventual winners Bolton Wanderers. Back in the First Division, Roy was allowed to move to Leicester after scoring in Blackburn's 4-1 home win over Burnley (see match report, pages 90-91). After one season with the Foxes, Roy joined Alf Ramsey's misfits at Ipswich. Second Division Champions in 1961, they shook up the soccer world by pipping Burnley to the League Championship in their very first season in the top flight.

Roy was virtually an ever-present in the side where his scintillating wing play created many of the chances for an attack which notched over a century of goals on their way to the title. It must have been a deeply satisfying moment for Roy when he scored against Burnley who suffered a 6-2 thrashing at the hands of the 'Tractor Boys'.

Ewood Park, 7 March 1959. Roy Stephenson scores in Blackburn's 4-1 League win over Burnley.

John Connelly
Winger
Born: St Helens, 18 July 1938

During the Fifties and Sixties, Burnley produced a stream of international-class wingers and they did not come any better than John Connelly. He notched 20 goals and was the team's top scorer when they secured the League Championship in 1960. Two years later he was a key member of the side which finished runners-up in a double bid for the title and FA Cup.

Fast and direct, John could operate on either flank and achieved an excellent strike rate for a winger. While still an apprentice joiner and part-time professional, his impressive displays earned an England call-up for the first of 20 caps in 1959. Inevitably, Burnley could not resist a big-money offer from Manchester United in 1964. Playing in a forward line containing Law, Charlton and Best, John won another Championship medal with 'The Reds' and became an automatic choice for England's 1966 World Cup squad. Selected for the goalless opening match against Uruguay, John came closest to breaking the deadlock with a header which hit the bar, then found himself on the sidelines for the remainder of the competition as Alf Ramsey's 'wingless wonders' went on to defeat West Germany in the final.

Returning to Old Trafford, Matt Busby surprisingly made John available for transfer. Newly relegated Blackburn Rovers swooped to sign the winger while Burnley dithered over whether to re-sign their former star. Despite the club's failure to regain their status in the top flight, John gave outstanding service to Rovers before moving on to end a distinguished career with Bury. It is a tribute to his ability that he is regarded by supporters on each side of the East Lancashire divide to be one of the greatest players to grace Turf Moor or Ewood Park.

Ewood Park, 8 October 1960. Blackburn defenders Matt Woods and Fred Pickering close in on Burnley winger John Connelly.

Walter Joyce
Defender/Midfield
Born: Oldham,
   10 September 1937

Walter Joyce shields the ball from Willie Irvine at Turf Moor in October 1964.

Former captain of Lancashire Schoolboys, Walter Joyce turned professional with Burnley in 1954 and after National Service, rose through the junior teams to become a valued squad member during Burnley's glory years in the early 1960s. With the depth of talent available at Turf Moor, Walter had to fight hard for selection but his versatility enabled him to cover both flanks at wing half and full-back. Making his debut in 1960, Walter established himself at right half and played in every round of Burnley's FA Cup run which ended in the semi-final against Spurs. The following season, he found himself on the sidelines as the Clarets finished runners-up in the League and cup. Joining Blackburn in 1964, Walter became a regular in the side which was relegated two years later and was then joined by former Clarets John Connelly and Adam Blacklaw, revelling in a midfield role as Rovers vainly attempted to regain their status in the top flight.

Moving to finish his playing days with home town club Oldham in 1967, he later joined the coaching staff which was to be the first step of a successful career move at various clubs. In 1993, son Warren followed in his father's footsteps and caused quite a stir by scoring two goals on his League debut for Burnley.

Adam Blacklaw
Goalkeeper
Born: Aberdeen, 2 September 1937

A career-blighting injury to England goalkeeper Colin McDonald gave Adam Blacklaw an unexpected opportunity to establish himself in the first team in March 1959. It was his good fortune that Burnley were about to enter a golden period in their history and challenge for the top honours. In his first full season between the posts Burnley won the League Championship and qualified for the European Cup, then followed up this success by reaching the 1962 FA Cup final at Wembley.

The former Schoolboy International had made his Burnley debut in 1956 but was restricted to a handful of appearances by the form of his illustrious predecessor. However, he soon proved his ability with his command of the area and spectacular style which won Adam many admirers among the Turf Moor faithful. The 'keeper missed only two games in five seasons and his consistent performances caught the eye of the Scottish selectors. Yet, despite winning his third full cap in a World Cup qualifying match against Italy in January 1966, he was no longer an automatic choice for his club with Harry Thompson vying for the green jersey. In July 1967, Burnley accepted an offer of £15,000 from neighbours Blackburn. At Ewood Park he took over from Fred Else and linked up with Burnley old boys Walter Joyce and John Connelly as the club struggled in the old Second Division. After making a century of appearances for the blue and whites, Adam moved on to his third Lancashire club at Blackpool where once again Harry Thompson barred the way to the first team. After playing only one game for The Seasiders, Adam pulled the curtain down on a fine career and retired.

Ewood Park, 8 October 1960. Burnley 'keeper Adam Blacklaw takes a high cross as skipper Jimmy Adamson and Chris Crowe challenge for the ball.

Keith Newton
Full-Back
Born: Manchester, 23 June 1941

Agreat servant to both East Lancashire clubs, Keith Newton began his professional career at Ewood Park in 1958. Converted from inside forward to full-back, his cool defensive qualities and overlapping runs down the flank soon marked him out for international honours. Winning his first cap in 1965, an injury-haunted season, which also resulted in Rovers dropping out of the top flight, contributed to keep him out of England's World Cup-winning squad. Merseyside giants Everton obtained Keith's signature in December 1969 and the club immediately won the League Championship. An automatic choice for the 1970 World Cup in Mexico, he emerged as a defender of the highest class. Two years later, Everton gave him a free transfer and Burnley snapped up the thirty-year-old as a ready-made replacement for long-serving John Angus, who had announced his retirement. Keith was an ever-present in his first season at Turf Moor when the team swept to the Second Division Championship and he continued to serve the club until released in 1978. Settling and working in Blackburn, it was a shock to all the friends he had made among the supporters of both East Lancashire clubs when Keith passed away only twenty years later.

Kevin Hird
Defender/Midfield
Born: Colne, 11 February 1955

Burnley scouts overlooked the talented local youngster who supported the club and Kevin Hird was given his chance at Ewood Park where he became an apprentice professional. Breaking into the first team in 1974, during Blackburn's Third Division Championship season, he established himself in the side but following the club's drop back to the Third Division, it was evident that a big club would come in for him. The future looked rosy when former Burnley great Jimmy Adamson, then managing Leeds United, paid a record fee for a full-back to take the defender to Elland Road in March 1979. Kevin was soon playing on the big stage alongside former Burnley stars Brian Flynn and Ray Hankin in Leeds' UEFA Cup campaign, but following Adamson's departure from the club a year later, the team went into decline and were relegated in 1982. Two years later, Kevin joined Burnley on a free transfer and settled into a side doomed to relegation. Despite Kevin's fine contribution, scoring 21 League and cup goals from midfield, the club were consigned to the Fourth Division for the first time in their history. After one season in the basement League, financial constraints resulted in the termination of his contract and Kevin plumped for non-League soccer, turning out for his hometown team Colne Dynamoes.

RECORDS OF PLAYERS WHO HAVE PLAYED FOR BOTH CLUBS

Name	BURNLEY Played	Apps	Goals	BLACKBURN Played	Apps	Goals
James APPLEBY	1953-58	1	0	1958-59	2	0
Eric BINNS	1949-55	15	0	1955-56	23	0
Adam BLACKLAW	1954-67	383	0	1967-70	110	0
Jack BRUTON	1925-29	176	44	1929-43	324	108
Marshall BURKE	1977-80	24	0	1980-82	43	8
Edgar CHADWICK	1899-00	32	10	1887-88	4*	3
Paul COMSTIVE	1987-89	110	25	1979-82	51	1
John CONNELLY	1956-64	265	105	1966-70	164	39
Wilf CROMPTON	1932-34	35	8	1927-32	20	5
Arthur CUNLIFFE	1937-38	9	0	1930-33	140	55
Peter DEVINE	1984-86	60	10	1982-84	8	2
David HAMILTON	1990-91	26	1	1981-85	123	7
Kevin HIRD	1984-86	105	31	1973-79	160	21
Harry JACKSON	1945-46	2*	1	1948-49	1	0
Lenny JOHNROSE	1999-02	50	4	1988-92	50	12
Walter JOYCE	1954-64	89	3	1964-67	135	4
Andy MARRIOTT	1990-91	17	0	1989-90	2	0
David MAY	2003-04	39	1	1988-94	151	6
James McEVELEY	2003-04+	5	0	2002-	15	1
Keith NEWTON	1972-78	252	7	1958-69	357	10
Tom NICOL	1891-96	149	44	1896-97	19	2
Peter O'DOWD	1930-31	67	8	1926-30	51	0
John PRICE	1960-65	22	2	1971-74	84	12
Ron SEWELL	1913-20	23	0	1920-27	248	0
Roy STEPHENSON	1949-56	80	28	1957-59	27	5
Levy THORPE	1913-20	79	5	1920-22	92	1
Andy TODD	2003-04+	8	1	2002-	35	1
Peter TURNBULL	1893-95	48	21	1895-96 (2 spells)		
				1897-98	27	8

* FA Cup appearances only
+ On loan

WARTIME MATCHES [appearances in brackets]

Blackburn's Albert Cowell (5), John Orr (5) and Albert Walmsley (21) made appearances for Burnley during the First World War.

Burnley's Allan Brown (2), Arthur Woodruff (1), Harold Rudman (1), Tom Gardner (3) and Bob Brocklebank (1) made 'guest' appearances for Blackburn during the Second World War.

During the First World War, future Huddersfield player and England international Sam Wadsworth played as an amateur for Rovers (7) and ended his League career at Burnley.

During the Second World War, Jack Chew played as an amateur for Rovers (23) before turning professional with Burnley.

EAST LANCASHIRE DREAM TEAM

Adam Blacklaw

Keith Newton   Peter O'Dowd   Levy Thorpe   Sam Wadsworth

Roy Stephenson   Kevin Hird   Edgar Chadwick

Arthur Cunliffe   Jack Bruton   John Connelly

Subs: Ron Sewell, Gilbert Walmsley, Walter Joyce, Jack Chew, Tom Nico

This fantasy squad contains nine full internationals: goalkeepers Ronnie Sewell and Adam Blacklaw; defenders Sam Wadsworth, Peter O'Dowd and Keith Newton and forwards Edgar Chadwick, Jack Bruton, Arthur Cunliffe and John Connelly. East Lancashire supporters must have wished such quality and depth could have been assembled during the turbulent years of the 1970s and 1980s. 'Flying Scot' Adam Blacklaw is selected for the starting line-up, covered by a back four which includes a pairing of classy full-backs in Keith Newton and Sam Wadsworth flanking ball-playing central defenders Peter O'Dowd and Levy Thorpe. The blend of midfield trio Roy Stephenson, Kevin Hird and Edgar Chadwick would create chances aplenty for attacking wingers Arthur Cunliffe and John Connelly. Jack Bruton's prolific goalscoring record from the wing would shame many centre forwards, therefore he is chosen to lead the attack in an effort to emulate Burnley wing-partner Louis Page who was similarly converted and immediately scored a double hat-trick. If the tactic should fail, player/manager Bruton can call upon a proven scorer in Tom Nicol who waits in reserve alongside 'keeper Ronnie Sewell; defenders Albert Walmsley, Walter Joyce and winger Jackie Chew.

During season 1967/68, these four 'derby doubles' lined up in the same team for Blackburn Rovers. From left to right: Keith Newton, John Connelly, Adam Blacklaw, Walter Joyce.

East Lancs Dream Team

Adam Blacklaw

Keith Newton   Peter O'Dowd   Levy Thorpe   Sam Wadsworth

Roy Stephenson   Kevin Hird   Edgar Chadwick

Arthur Cunliffe   Jack Bruton   John Connelly

4

LEAGUE TUSSLES

Turf Moor, 18 October 1958. Burnley 'keeper Colin McDonald watches a header from Ally MacLeod go wide in this goalless draw. From the eighty-two League meetings between the clubs this chapter presents a selection which were crucial to promotion and relegation issues.

FIRST DIVISION   23 APRIL 1898
BURNLEY 2   BLACKBURN ROVERS 0
Attendance: 12,000

The Football League banished automatic promotion and relegation and devised an early play-off system which involved the bottom two clubs in the First Division facing the top two teams from the Second Division in a mini-League of Test Matches. This situation produced an intriguing derby when Blackburn (second from bottom in the First Division) were drawn home and away against Burnley (top of the Second Division). The East Lancashire clubs would then face either Stoke or Newcastle and the outcome would determine which two clubs had gained enough points to attain First Division status. Burnley had fallen foul of this procedure the previous season when they were relegated for the first time.

A Wilf Toman hat-trick had given Burnley a flying start in a convincing 3-1 victory at Ewood Park (see match report, pages 14-15). For the return, the Clarets fielded the same team, while Rovers made four changes in a frantic effort to salvage something from a disastrous campaign. In the first half, Burnley 'keeper Jack Hillman only handled the ball once, while his Rovers counterpart James Carter was the busiest man on the field. Due to his brilliance, the Burnley forwards were denied time and again, leaving the visitors to count themselves extremely fortunate to reach the interval without having conceded a goal. Early in the second half, Burnley briefly lost the services of winger Tom 'Ching' Morrison, who resumed after treatment to an injured hand – suffered in what was described by the press as an off-the-ball 'bout' with marker Ted Killeen! In the fifty-third minute, he contributed to the opening goal when he linked up with Wilf Toman to provide a half-chance for Jimmy Ross. The inside right finally broke Carter's defiant resistance with a stunning shot into the top corner of the net from long range. Under constant pressure, the 'keeper continued to keep the Clarets at bay until blotting his copybook ten minutes from time. A fluffed goal kick landed at the feet of centre forward Wilf Toman who wrapped up the game by slamming the ball past the mortified custodian. Throughout the match, Rovers had only threatened from free-kicks, which were awarded in profusion to both sides as a result of over-zealous challenges in a keenly contested derby. There might have been dismissals but for the calm authoritative conduct of the referee who never let the situation get out of hand.

In the next stage of the Test matches, Burnley suffered a setback with a home defeat by Stoke. A whiff of scandal then hit soccer when the two teams came to 'a gentleman's agreement' after realising that a draw in their return match would ensure both clubs the point they required to book a place in the top division. Supporters jeered while watching a farcical exhibition of non-effort which went down in the annals of soccer history as 'The Game Without a Shot

Burnley scorer Jimmy Ross.

at Goal'. Fortunately, the other teams did not lose out through this blatant case of match-fixing because at the following Football League AGM, clubs adopted Burnley's proposal to retain Newcastle and Blackburn – despite Rovers' representative, founder John Lewis, stoically standing by his beliefs and opposing the motion to increase the number of teams in the First Division! The meeting also signalled the death knell of Test Matches which were jettisoned in favour of automatic promotion and relegation. It would be almost a hundred years before play-offs were reintroduced – this time on a strictly knock-out basis!

Burnley (2-3-5)

Jack Hillman; Jerry Reynolds, Tom McLintock; David Beveridge, Joe Taylor, Archie Livingstone; Tom Morrison, Jimmy Ross, Wilf Toman, Bill Bowes, Walter Place jnr. Secretary: Harry Bradshaw.

Blackburn Rovers (2-3-5)

James Carter; John Glover, Ted Killeen; Harry Marshall, Geordie Anderson, Kelly Houlker; John Moreland, Josh Hargreaves, John Proudfoot, John Wilkie, John Campbell. Secretary: Joseph Walmsley.

FIRST DIVISION   1 JANUARY 1900
BLACKBURN ROVERS 2   BURNLEY 0
Attendance: 14,000

The dawn of the twentieth century found both East Lancashire rivals facing the prospect of relegation which could be eased by gaining maximum points from this New Year's Day derby. Two days earlier, Burnley had beaten bottom club Glossop to boost their confidence and the possibility of completing the double over Blackburn, who had succumbed to the only goal of the match in an early season encounter at Turf Moor. However, the Clarets were to plumb new depths in their worst display of the season. Many of their followers were to regret making the short journey to Ewood Park, where they had the galling experience of witnessing their team surrender to a side reduced to ten men for three-quarters of the game.

Anxiety seemed to affect the finishing of the visitors, who wasted good chances to go ahead in the early stages. Left-winger Walter Place was the first culprit, blasting his shot high over the bar when in the clear. His counterpart on the right, Richard Hannigan, then wasted a fine move by Tom Morrison and Edgar Chadwick, failing to make contact with a pass when he only had 'keeper Albert Knowles to beat. The Clarets could not even capitalise on Rovers' misfortune midway through the half when Dan Hurst came off worse in a collision with his teammate Jack Dewhurst. When the 'magic sponge' failed to revive him, the injured winger was carried from the field and was unable to take any further part in the match. Unperturbed by this setback, Rovers immediately took the lead through the shaken Dewhurst, who collected a through ball from half-back Sam McClure, before beating 'keeper Jack Hillman with a powerful drive. Blackburn went further ahead shortly after the interval from a corner. Rovers' outstanding player, centre half Tom Booth, sent in a powerful header which was parried by Jack Hillman, before inside right Tom Briercliffe reacted quickly to fire home the rebound. Confidence visibly drained from the visitors who found themselves under constant pressure from a depleted forward line for the remainder of the game. A heavier defeat was only avoided by the superb goalkeeping of Jack Hillman who topped a great display with a miraculous save to deny centre forward Ben Hulse in the last minute.

Alarm bells were now ringing for the Turfites with 'Sportsman' of the *Burnley Express* giving an ominous warning: 'The game was one of the poorest in which Burnley have participated for some time, and the feeling of many of those who undertook the journey was that all danger of a drop to the Second Division and ultimate extinction is not passed.' In fact, the relegation issue was not resolved until the very last match of the season. With Glossop doomed, it was possible they might be joined by any one of four teams above them: Burnley, Preston, Notts County and Blackburn Rovers. The permutations were increased by a quirk of the fixture list which brought Preston and Blackburn together. Burnley

Jack Hillman – a miraculous save.

vainly went in search of points at Nottingham Forest, who did their derby rivals County a favour by scoring four goals without reply. The result left Rovers sure of avoiding the drop and the Clarets had a futile two-day wait to see if their neighbours could save them by beating Preston, but it was not to be. Burnley were consigned to the Second Division where they would remain for thirteen years before resurrecting their fortunes.

Blackburn Rovers (2-3-5)
Albert Knowles; Tom Brandon, Bob Crompton; Sam McClure, Tom Booth, Robert Haworth; James Law, Tom Briercliffe, Ben Hulse, Jack Dewhurst, Dan Hurst.
Secretary: Joseph Walmsley.

Burnley (2-3-5)
Jack Hillman; Tom Woolfall, Tom McLintock; Fred Barron, Joe Taylor, Archie Livingstone; Richard Hannigan, Tom Morrison, Edgar Chadwick, Walter Place snr, John Miller.
Secretary: Ernest Mangnall.

FIRST DIVISION   8 SEPTEMBER 1913
BURNLEY 1   BLACKBURN ROVERS 2
Attendance : 36,000

The East Lancashire rivals had been parted in the League following Burnley's relegation at the turn of the century. The thirteenth attempt to climb out of the Second Division proved lucky for the Clarets who were promoted as runners-up behind Preston North End. During the successful campaign, appetites for the return of derby action had been whetted when Burnley eliminated Rovers on their way to the semi-final of the FA Cup (see match report, pages 38-39). Blackburn had an early opportunity to avenge their cup exit in this eagerly anticipated encounter. Turf Moor officials announced record gate receipts which would have been considerably increased had large numbers of people not gained free admission by entering the ground via the cricket club entrance. Most of the crowd were assembled before the Blackburn team made a late arrival and were forced to change hurriedly in order to make a punctual start.

Rovers skipper Bob Crompton won the toss and chose to play with the wind blowing from the Cricketfield End. Despite an enterprising start by the visitors, it was the Clarets who took an early lead in the fourth minute, with a slick move created by Billy Nesbitt. The winger made a darting run down the right, before checking back inside a defender, then floated over a cross which was deftly laid back by Ted Hodgson into the path of centre forward Bert Freeman who drove the ball past helpless 'keeper Alf Robinson. The home side went close to increasing their lead when a chip from Hodgson ran along the crossbar before dropping behind for a goal-kick. The Clarets' defence then came under increasing pressure and conceded three corners in quick succession. Rovers snatched an equaliser from the third of these, conceded by 'keeper Jerry Dawson, who pushed a shot from winger Jock Simpson around the post. Joe Hodgkinson took the corner from the left and in the ensuing goalmouth scramble, centre half Percy Smith fired home from close range in the thirty-fifth minute. Burnley were then reduced to ten men, when defender David Taylor left the field for lengthy treatment to a cut knee, which required stitches before he resumed after the interval. Blackburn scored the winner only four minutes into the second half. Rovers' best forward Eddie Latherton was fouled on the edge of the penalty area and found George Chapman with the free-kick. The centre forward was surrounded by defenders and had little room to manoeuvre, but did brilliantly to turn and squeeze the ball into the net. Burnley fought hard to level the scores and won several corners, without penetrating a solid defence. Late in the game, the visitors broke away and should have extended their lead when Latherton missed the best chance of the match.

A goalless draw was played out in the return derby at Ewood Park on New Year's Day. Both clubs had an outstanding season and shared the top domestic

War casualty Eddie Latherton.

honours. For the second time in three years, Blackburn Rovers clinched the League Championship, while Burnley consolidated their place in the top flight and carried off the FA Cup. A glorious era for Blackburn and Burnley was curtailed after one more season when they finished third and fourth respectively, before derby 'battles' became secondary to the real thing in war-torn Europe. Players answered the call to arms and Blackburn's England international Eddie Latherton went off to Fance and tragically lost his life at the Front in 1917.

Burnley (2-3-5)
Jerry Dawson; Tom Bamford, David Taylor; George Halley, Tommy Boyle, Billy Watson; Billy Nesbitt, Dick Lindley, Bert Freeman, Ted Hodgson, Bill Husband.
Manager: John Haworth.

Blackburn Rovers (2-3-5)
Alf Robinson; Bob Crompton, Arthur Cowell; Albert Walmsley, Percy Smith, Billy Bradshaw; Jock Simpson, Danny Shea, George Chapman, Eddie Latherton, Joe Hodkinson. Manager: Robert Middleton.

FIRST DIVISION   15 JANUARY 1921
BURNLEY 4   BLACKBURN ROVERS 1
Attendance: 41,534

Burnley had experienced a poor start, losing the first three games of the campaign, before transforming their season in spectacular style. They came into this derby hoping to chalk up their twentieth game without defeat. Brimming with confidence, the table-topping Clarets put out the same team for the twelfth consecutive game, while their mid-table rivals had selection problems, caused by injuries to key players and were forced to field a team containing five reserves. Making a welcome return to Turf Moor were former Clarets Ron Sewell and Levy Thorpe who had been transferred to Blackburn the previous season. The crowd were treated to some pre-match amusement by the antics of a pet monkey that was released onto the pitch at the Cricketfield end of the ground. The home side were soon making 'monkeys' of the visitors, whose depleted team were completely outclassed by the League leaders.

From the outset, the Burnley attack tore into the opposition and it came as no surprise when forward Benny Cross shot the Clarets ahead after 15 minutes. He took a pass from left-winger Walter Weaver and beat 'keeper Ron Sewell with a blistering drive from twenty-five yards. Rovers fought back and equalised in the thirty-eighth minute when Billy Sandman beat two defenders before giving 'keeper Jerry Dawson no chance from an oblique angle. The centre forward's impressive debut was brought to an abrupt end during the next attack when a crude challenge from full-back Len Smelt brought him crashing, leaving him with a painful knee injury which severely diminished his effectiveness for the remainder of the game. It was also obvious that full-back Jim Donnelly was carrying a leg injury. To add to their woes, Rovers fell behind just before the break when Bob Kelly fired home a cross-shot from the edge of the area which Sewell failed to stop despite getting a hand to the ball.

It was Burnley all the way after the interval as they produced delightful flowing football, with effortless passing and movement which tied the opposition in knots. Blackburn were rarely threatening, although Jerry Dawson had to be at his best to keep out two shots from former teammate Levy Thorpe. Rovers 'keeper Ron Sewell conceded more than two goals in a match for the first time that season when the home side went further ahead midway through the second period. Benny Cross collected his second goal of the match following good work by wing half Billy Watson. The Clarets asserted their superiority when skipper Tommy Boyle joined in the attack and fired home a screamer from long range. Burnley's Walter Weaver limped off with an ankle injury ten minutes from the end but it was too late to affect the result as the Clarets took the derby in convincing fashion. The superiority of the victors was underlined by 'Rover', 'Their understanding and positional play, as is perhaps only natural in a team which has played unchanged for practically three

Benny Cross – two goals for Burnley.

months, was streets ahead of that of Rovers, whose efforts seemed most puny by comparison.'

A week later, the Clarets journeyed to Ewood Park and completed the double over a Rovers team back at full strength. They then went on to clinch the League Championship, going one better than the season before when they had finished in second spot. After thirty matches their record League run came to an end when they were defeated at Maine Road by eventual runners-up Manchester City. Quickly recovering from this temporary setback, Burnley completed the campaign in style having suffered only four losses in forty-two league games.

Burnley (2-3-5)
Jerry Dawson; Len Smelt, Cliff Jones; George Halley, Tommy Boyle, Billy Watson; Billy Nesbitt, Bob Kelly, Joe Anderson, Benny Cross, Walter Weaver.
Manager: John Haworth.

Blackburn Rovers (2-3-5)
Ron Sewell; Jim Donnelly, Joe Bibby; Levy Thorpe, Frank Reilly, Tom Heaton; Joe Hodkinson, Peter Holland, Billy Sandham, Ernie Hawksworth, Bill McCall.
Manager: Robert Middleton.

FIRST DIVISION   15 MARCH 1930
BURNLEY 3   BLACKBURN ROVERS 2
Attendance: 16,673

Earlier in the season, Burnley had suffered their greatest reverse at the hands of Blackburn Rovers, losing 8-3 at Ewood Park (see match report, pages 28-29). In the return at Turf Moor, not only was it important to avenge this humiliation, but the Clarets desperately needed maximum points as they were staring relegation in the face with an abysmal record of only one win from their last ten matches. In contrast, Rovers came into this match looking certain of a top-six finish, having just lost their first game in seven against eventual League runners-up Derby County. Wintry conditions were not conducive to good football, but supporters who braved the arctic cold were rewarded with an excellent spectacle in a keenly fought contest. Lining up against each other since their transfers in opposite directions between the clubs were Blackburn winger Jack Bruton and Burnley centre half Peter O'Dowd who, in the previous meeting, had faced each other on different sides of the derby fence.

Prospects did not look promising for the home side in the opening period. They lost the toss and had to face the wind and driving sleet, then suffered injuries to full-back Andy McCluggage and inside forward Tom Prest who both struggled on to complete the game. Rovers made the most of these advantages when they went ahead after thirty-four minutes through Tom McLean, whose shot struck full-back Jim Brown and was deflected past stranded 'keeper George Sommerville. Within four minutes, the Clarets were back on level terms courtesy of an own goal. A high cross from winger Louis Page swirled under the bar and unfortunate 'keeper Cliff Binns caught the ball as he inadvertently stepped over the line. Rovers wasted numerous chances to restore their lead until finally succeeding in the dying moments of the first half when centre forward Clarrie Bourton survived an offside appeal to drive home a well-delivered cross from left-winger Arthur Cunliffe.

Incredibly, the Clarets had equalised and taken the lead within two minutes of the resumption. Limping Burnley skipper Andy McCluggage shook off the discomfort of bruising to his chest and stepped up to convert a penalty, after handball had been harshly awarded against centre half Bill Rankin, who blocked a fierce drive from Page. Burnley pivot Peter O'Dowd then capped an outstanding display by scoring the winner against his old teammates. He cracked home a direct free-kick which had been awarded after forward Jim Wallace had been brought down by full-back Jock Hutton. From this point, Burnley totally dominated the game and their opponents had Cliff Binns to thank for 'keeping' the score respectable with a string of fine saves. Rovers might have salvaged a point when Tommy McLean got a late chance to add to his tally but shot weakly straight at Sommerville.

Peter O'Dowd scored the
winner against his former club.

A relieved *Burnley Express* reporter hoped that this result would lift the Clarets out of the doldrums, 'I have hopes that the victory, apart from the fact that it was a victory over the Rovers and in some respects a revenge for the heavy defeat at Ewood Park earlier in the season, will have far greater effect. No victory ever came at a more opportune tme'. Unfortunately, Burnley's revival was short-lived, although they went into the last game of the season with a slim chance of avoiding relegation. Second-placed Derby County were thrashed 6-2 at Turf Moor, but it was not enough as the Clarets unluckily finished second from bottom, level on points with Sheffield Wednesday who were saved by a superior goal average.

Burnley (2-3-5)
George Sommerville; Andy McCluggage, George Waterfield; Jim Brown, Peter O'Dowd, Alex Forrest; Joe Mantle, Tom Prest, George Beel, Jim Wallace, Louis Page. Manager: Albert Pickles.

Blackburn Rovers (2-3-5)
Cliff Binns; Jock Hutton, Herbert Jones; Bill Imrie, Bill Rankin, Jack Roscamp; Jack Bruton, Syd Puddefoot, Clarrie Bourton, Tommy McLean, Arthur Cunliffe. Manager: Bob Crompton.

SECOND DIVISION

27 FEBRUARY 1937

BLACKBURN ROVERS 3

BURNLEY 1

Attendance: 18,240

Blackburn Rovers' relegation to the Second Division for the first time in their history brought together the old rivals in League action after an absence of six years. A goalless draw had resulted in the earlier encounter at Turf Moor and the teams lined up for the return in freezing wet weather, which had an understandable affect on the attendance. However, the home club's loss of gate money was adequately compensated for by a resounding victory over their neighbours.

A stamina-sapping game, played in torrential rain and clinging mud, took its toll on a Burnley side that had been trounced in the fifth round of the FA Cup by Arsenal a week earlier, before bouncing back to beat Second Division leaders Blackpool – only three days before facing the daunting prospect of an away trip for an East Lancashire derby. The visitors showed no signs of weariness in the early stages and adapted to the gluepot conditions well, making intelligent use of the firmer ground on the flanks where wingers Jimmy Stein and Charlie Fletcher made dangerous raids against a shaky-looking defence. On one occasion, Rovers' full-back Ernie Lanceley sliced the ball inches over the bar attempting to make a hurried clearance. The Clarets deservedly went ahead after seventeen minutes when the wingers combined for Stein to head home Fletcher's corner. Rovers responded straight from the restart and Len Butt put the ball in the net but was penalised for using his hand. However, the same forward got on the scoresheet after thirty-three minutes when he ran through the Burnley defence to draw 'keeper Ted Adams out before beating him with a low drive into the corner. Burnley went close to retaking the lead when 'keeper Hughes made a fine one-handed save to turn away a high cross-shot from Fletcher.

The tide gradually turned in Rovers' favour after the break. Their defence tightened, shored up admirably by the imposing presence of centre half Bob Pryde who was dominant in the air and sure-footed with anything he had to deal with on the ground. It was now the turn of the Blackburn wingers Jack Bruton and Bill Guest to show their mettle. Former Claret Bruton took a superb pass from wing half Arnold Whiteside to put Rovers ahead in the sixty-third minute, hitting a long-range shot which deceived the 'keeper after taking a deflection off full-back Alex Robinson. With three minutes remaining, Guest also got in on the act, racing onto a through ball inside the full-back from Charlie Calladine before coolly placing his shot past the advancing Adams to make certain of the points.

Blackburn had finished the more determined team, typified by their best player Len Butt who kept his sleeves rolled-up in the atrocious conditions. His attitude was in stark contrast to the bedraggled Burnley team seemingly at the

Len Butt scored the equaliser.

limit of their endurance who, according to sports reporter 'Rover', trooped off the pitch looking like 'a badly beaten boat race crew'. To add to their misery, the visitors made their way back home during the worst snowfall of the winter and recovered to complete the season in mid-table, just one place above Rovers, who disappointingly failed in their ambition to regain their First Division status at the first attempt.

Blackburn Rovers (2-3-5)

Jack Hughes; Ernie Lancely, Walter Crook; Arnold Whiteside, Bob Pryde, John Wightman; Jack Bruton, Len Butt, Tommy Sale, Charlie Calladine, Billy Guest. Manager: Reg Taylor.

Burnley (2-3-5)

Ted Adams; Gilbert Richmond, Alex Robinson; Frank Rayner, Arthur Woodruff, Bill Smith; Jimmy Stein, Peter Fisher, John Gastall, Billy Miller, Charlie Fletcher. Manager: Alf Boland.

SECOND DIVISION   15 OCTOBER 1938

BURNLEY 3   BLACKBURN ROVERS 2

Attendance: 29,254

Thrills rather than frills were the order of the day as a string of amazing blunders committed in attack and defence by Blackburn Rovers were the decisive factor which presented the points to their old rivals in this derby tussle. Nevertheless, right up to the final whistle, the outcome was always in doubt, as the teams were locked in an exhilarating struggle which had more twists and turns than the murky canal that winds its way between the two mill-towns.

The Clarets were two up within seventeen minutes. They took a surprise lead in the second minute when Rovers' winger Bobby Langton stretched to keep in a long clearance he could have left to claim a throw-in. The ball ran into the path of Tom Garner who pounced and made rapid ground along the flank before releasing an accurate centre to centre forward Jim Clayton who beat 'keeper Jim Barron with a hard low drive. Wing half Gardner was to the fore again when he initiated a fine move to put the home side further ahead. With raking strides he cut through the Rovers' defence toward the left before switching play with a clever reverse pass to Fred Taylor. The winger swung over a high cross which Clayton headed home from the edge of the area with prodigious power. Blackburn's concerted attempts to reduce the arrears went unrewarded before the interval, although they missed a golden chance in the dying moments when Albert Clarke headed inches wide from a good position.

Within five minutes of the restart Clarke made amends with a great individual effort. He dribbled along the edge of the box before suddenly shooting past 'keeper Ted Adams through a circle of defenders. Rovers upped the tempo in search of an equaliser but made two astonishing misses from close range. Firstly, winger Billy Rogers somehow contrived to scoop the ball over the bar when the ball dropped invitingly to him on the near post, then Jack Weddle flicked a low cross wide of an unguarded goal from only a yard out. Midway through the half, Jim Clayton thought he had sewn the game up for the Clarets, but he was denied a hat-trick when the referee awarded a goal, then changed his mind and gave offside, after being persuaded to consult the linesman. Two minutes later, the visitors continued their revival with a well-deserved leveller when Clarke climbed above the defence to head his second from a well-judged cross delivered by inside right Len Butt. The pendulum now appeared to be swinging in Rovers' favour but they were the architects of their own downfall when a comedy of errors led to Burnley snatching a winner in the closing minutes. Bobby Langton collected a loose ball in space but put his defence under pressure with a poor back pass which wing half Frank Chilvers sliced across the goal mouth. Jim Barron and Billy Hough then got in a tangle and failed to clear the danger, allowing the ball to run to winger

Second Division Champions 1939. From left to right, back row: Bob Crompton (manager), Walter Crook, Bob Pryde, Arnold Whiteside, Jimmy Barron, Frank Chivers, Ernest Lanceley. Front row: Billy Rogers, Len Butt, Jock Weddle, Albert Clarke, Bobby Langton.

Ron Hornby, who could hardly believe his luck as he gleefully accepted the gift.

This disappointing result was the third League defeat in a row for Blackburn, but they quickly turned around their season and finished on a high note, beating Burnley in the return on their way to winning the Second Division Championship. It marked a triumphant return to Ewood Park for manager Bob Crompton, but gathering war clouds meant that the club's elevation to the top flight would have to be put on hold for the duration. Sadly, two lynch pins of Blackburn's success, Albert Clarke and Frank Chivers would lose their lives during the conflict.

Burnley (2-3-5)
Ted Adams; Alex Robinson, Tom Chester; Tom Gardner, Robert Johnson, George Bray; Fred Taylor, Billy Miller, Jim Clayton, Bob Brocklebank, Ron Hornby.
Manager: Alf Boland.

Blackburn Rovers (2-3-5)
Jim Barron; Billy Hough, Walter Crook; Arnold Whiteside, Bob Pryde, Frank Chivers; Billy Rogers, Len Butt, Jack Weddle, Albert Clarke, Bobby Langton.
Manager: Bob Crompton.

FIRST DIVISION	18 OCTOBER 1947
BLACKBURN ROVERS 1	BURNLEY 2
Attendance: 41,635	

When the Second World War came to a peaceful conclusion, the Football League resumed hostilities and Blackburn Rovers took their long-awaited place in the top flight after emerging as Second Division Champions in 1939. They were soon joined by Burnley who had an outstanding season, reaching the 1947 FA Cup final and clinching promotion to set up this first post-war League meeting between the derby rivals.

The match got off to a disastrous start for Rovers when they gifted a goal to the opposition in the second minute. Defender Bob Tomlinson cut out a cross from the right, but under pressure from winger Jack Hays, attempted a hurried backpass to 'keeper George Marks who was advancing off his line as the ball sailed over his head into an unguarded net. With the taunts of the home supporters spurring them on, Rovers fought back and took control of the game but were thwarted by a resolute defence marshalled by Burnley skipper Allan Brown. Winger Bobby Langton was a constant threat and sent over several dangerous crosses which custodian Jimmy Strong did well to cut out. When the 'keeper was beaten, Allan Brown and George Bray covered well to clear point-blank shots off the line as Rovers went in at the interval still searching for an equaliser.

Incredibly, minutes after the restart, Blackburn repeated their earlier mistake. Full-back George Higgins was caught in two minds and made a fatal hesitation which allowed Billy Morris to gather the ball and race through the defence before drawing Marks and slotting the ball wide of the 'keeper for the second goal. The home side's dominance was undone by these costly errors, but undaunted they strove bravely on and reduced the arrears when winger Jackie Oakes intercepted a pass from Harry Potts and sped down the touchline before hitting over an accurate cross to Alec Venters who gave Jimmy Strong no chance from close range. The Burnley attack tried hard to restore their two-goal cushion. Firts, former Blackburn amateur Jack Chew, then fellow forward Jack Billingham, both went close with efforts which scraped the crossbar. The best chance to put the result beyond doubt fell once more to Billingham who was put clean through by Billy Morris, but failed to capitalise on a golden opportunity by firing wide with only Marks to beat. As tensions rose, the game came to an unseemly end when Blackburn pivot Bob Pryde was involved in an unpleasant incident with Harry Potts which left the Burnley forward writhing in agony on the ground. In a time when match officials were more tolerant and dismissals extremely rare, the pair were decidedly lucky to stay on the field and the referee did not even reach for his book, preferring instead to issue a stern lecture.

The return match at Turf Moor ended in a goalless draw and Burnley consolidated their position in the First Division with a impressive third-place

Billy Morris scored Burnley's second.

finish, while Rovers floundered and were relegated after one win in their last ten games consigned them to the Second Divison. Manager Will Scott had succumbed to ill-health after only three games and handed over the reins to former Burnley and Blackburn player Jack Bruton who could not reverse the club's fortunes. It would be ten long years before Rovers built a team capable of climbing back to rejoin their neighbours in the top flight.

Blackburn Rovers (2-3-5)

George Marks; Bob Tomlinson, George Higgins; Jimmy Baldwin, Bob Pryde, Eric Bell; Jackie Oakes, Les Graham, Verdi Godwin, Alec Venters, Bobby Langton.
Manager: Will Scott.

Burnley (2-3-5)

Jim Strong; Arthur Woodruff, Harold Mather; Reg Atwell, Allan Brown, George Bray; Jack Chew, Bill Morris, John Billingham, Harry Potts, Jack Hays.
Manager: Cliff Britton.

FIRST DIVISION   7 MARCH 1959

BLACKBURN ROVERS 4   BURNLEY 1

Attendance: 27,071

Following Blackburn's elevation from the Second Division, the first League derby in ten years between the old rivals had ended in a scoreless draw at Turf Moor the previous October. To add spice to the season, the teams had been drawn together early in New Year to face each other in the fourth round of FA Cup when Burnley emerged victorious at Ewood Park (see match report, pages 42-43). This second League meeting gave Rovers the chance to avenge their elimination from the cup. Burnley came into the derby suffering from the hangover of a sixth-round cup exit inflicted in a replay four days earlier by 'bogey' team Aston Villa. Blackburn's Ronnie Clayton climbed out of his sick-bed to take his place in the line-up on the day that he had been selected as captain of the Football League. Also named in the side was Burnley goalkeeper Colin McDonald, who was omitted from this derby for reasons of ill health, but would recover to play against the League of Ireland – where he suffered the tragedy of a broken leg which ended his career.

With cheeky chappie Bryan Douglas at his tantalising, confident best, Rovers dominated the opening exchanges before the visitors scored the opener against the run of play after twenty minutes. A cross from John Connelly was pushed out by 'keeper Harry Leyland and centre forward Ray Pointer pounced on the clearance to slam the ball into the net. Rovers equalised after half an hour when Peter Dobing shot through a crowd of players to beat the unsighted Blacklaw, then the home side deservedly took the lead shortly before the interval when ex-Claret Roy Stephenson put one over his former teammates by converting a pass from centre forward Dobing. Blackburn should have made certain of the points by this stage but two gilt-edged chances were passed up by Roy Vernon which gave Burnley a chance to regroup and try an make amends in the second half.

For twenty minutes after the break, Rovers' defence looked decidedly jittery and should have been punished, but they were let off the hook by a surprisingly lacklustre Burnley team. Ray Pointer's wholehearted example as an indefatigable leader of the line could not inspire other members of the attack. When a goal was eventually scored, it was at the other end. It proved to be a dream debut for winger Jock Airey who finished off a good move by club stalwarts Ron Clayton and Bryan Douglas, which left him with the task of side-footing into the net for the simplest goal he would ever score. With neither side firing on all cylinders, the home supporters could not take a win for granted until the closing moments as Burnley continued to look dangerous on the break and threatened to close the gap. However, in a grandstand finish, Rovers emphasised the superiority they had shown throughout when Roy Vernon made up for his earlier misses by sewing up the game from an opportunity created by the hard-working Stephenson.

Burnley's Ray Pointer sprawls as he hits the ball past Harry Leyland and Matt Woods for the opening goal.

As for Burnley, they had just been too bad to be true and 'Centurion', writing in the *Blackburn Evening Telegraph*, warned readers: 'Restrained jubilation should be the keynote of any Rovers' celebrations of the 4-1 defeat of Burnley; there is no reason to drink the cellar dry. The Rovers deserved their revenge win – that is beyond question – but Burnley provided such poor opposition that the occasion was rather spoiled.'

Blackburn Rovers (2-3-5)

Harry Leyland; Ken Taylor, Dave Whelan; Ron Clayton, Matt Woods, Mick McGrath; Bryan Douglas, Roy Stephenson, Peter Dobing, Roy Vernon, Jock Airey.
Manager: Dally Duncan.

Burnley (2-3-5)

Adam Blacklaw; Tommy Cummings, Dave Smith; Bobby Seith, Brian Miller, Jimmy Adamson; John Connelly, Jimmy McIlroy, Ray Pointer, Jimmy Robson, Brian Pilkington.
Manager: Harry Potts.

FIRST DIVISION
BLACKBURN ROVERS 3
Attendance: 33,316

17 OCTOBER 1959
BURNLEY 2

'**D**efeat is inevitable at times, but when it is administered summarily by the feet of near neighbours it is apt to assume the aspect of a catastrophe of some sporting importance' wrote despondent reporter 'Sportsman' in the *Burnley Express* after the Clarets had lost this match by the odd goal in five. A draw would have perhaps been a fairer result, but Rovers were to prove a thorn in the side of Burnley's League and cup aspirations during a season which was to prove a high-water mark for the East Lancashire rivals as they each emerged as forerunners for top domestic honours.

As they lined up for the start, both teams were missing a star player called up for international duty. Blackburn's Ron Clayton was captaining his country for the first time following the retirement of Billy Wright. Under his 'wing' was Burnley's John Connelly, awarded his first England cap at the expense of Bryan Douglas. The omitted Rovers winger was obviously designated as the danger-man by the opposition, and full-back Alex Elder was given instructions to follow him everywhere. The results were comical as 'Duggie' wandered all over the pitch in a forlorn attempt to put space between himself and his dogged marker in an incident-packed game with tough tackling and no shortage of thrills. Blackburn forward Peter Dobing made the opening goal for the home side when he burst past three defenders and squared the ball for Derek Dougan to take the pass in his stride and beat 'keeper Adam Blacklaw with a tremendous shot. Burnley hit back when a cleverly worked free-kick by Bobby Seith and Jimmy McIlroy gave winger Brian Pilkington the opportunity to equalise. Speedy Peter Dobing broke through the Burnley defence again and with everyone expecting him to pass as before, surprised Blacklaw, beating him with a hard shot fired in at the near post from an acute angle. Blackburn were well on top and deserved their lead at this stage but presented the opposition with a gift goal early in the second half. Awarded a free-kick on the edge of the area, Burnley wing half Brian Miller turned the ball square to Bobby Seith whose shot cannoned off the wall to Bryan Douglas. The winger nonchalantly pushed a backpass towards 'keeper Harry Leyland, then clasped his head in horror as he watched the ball curl into the net. Now on level terms, it looked likely that the Clarets would go ahead against their dispirited rivals. The home goal had a number of fortuitous escapes before Rovers recovered to score a shock winner. Welsh international Roy Vernon floated a high free-kick over the wall into the area. Blacklaw came out confidently to take the catch but was apparently unsighted by the challenge of Dougan. Both players completely missed the ball which arched gently over them both into the net. In the dying moments, the Clarets were robbed of a point by the brilliance of 'keeper Harry Leyland

Goalkeeper Harry Leyland watches in horror as Rovers concede an own goal scored by Bryan Douglas (not in picture).

who made a superb double-save at point-blank range to earn his team a win bonus.

On their way to winning the League Championship, Burnley gained revenge for this defeat with a single-goal victory at Turf Moor. However, a week after the League return, the Clarets' hopes of a League and cup 'double' were cruelly dashed in a memorable sixth-round clash (see match reports, pages 44-47). Rovers overcame them after a replay on the way to becoming losing FA Cup finalists at Wembley.

Blackburn Rovers (2-3-5)

Harry Leyland; John Bray, Fred Pickering; Bill Smith, Matt Woods, Mick McGrath; Bryan Douglas, Peter Dobing, Derek Dougan, Roy Vernon, Ally MacLeod.
Manager: Dally Duncan.

Burnley (2-3-5)

Adam Blacklaw; John Angus, Alex Elder; Bobby Seith, Jimmy Adamson, Brian Miller; Brian Pilkington, Jimmy McIlroy, Ray Pointer, Billy White, Gordon Harris.
Manager: Harry Potts.

FIRST DIVISION	24 FEBRUARY 1962
BLACKBURN ROVERS 2	BURNLEY 1
Attendance: 33,914	

Fortunes seesawed in this thrilling derby at Ewood Park as top-of-the-table Burnley stumbled to their first defeat of the New Year against their struggling rivals. The Clarets had been in scintillating form and lined up having amassed an impressive 94 goals in 31 cup and League matches. They made an enforced change for this game with winger Ian Towers coming in for the injured Gordon Harris. The visitors were clearly the superior side in the first half and Rovers owed much to Fred Else for keeping them in the game. The custodian made superlative saves to deny a rampant Burnley attack. The highlight of his display was a brilliant one-handed save when Jimmy McIlroy lashed in a tremendous left-foot shot. Both teams had confident appeals for penalties turned down before Burnley took a well-deserved lead after twenty-seven minutes. John Connelly swung a corner over from the right which was back-headed at the near post by Ian Towers. As the ball flew across the face of goal, Ray Pointer timed his run superbly to climb above Blackburn skipper Matt Woods and thump home a header. The livewire centre forward was proving a handful for the Rovers defence. Just before the interval he also shook off the attention of a playful black dog that ran the danger of accompanying the ball in flight as a high cross found Jimmy Robson, who headed over the bar. The game was transformed in the opening minute of the restart when Rovers capitalised on a defensive blunder to snatch a confidence-boosting equaliser. Burnley 'keeper Adam Blacklaw and full-back Alex Elder got in a tangle and gave away an unnecessary corner. Bryan Douglas crossed to striker Fred Pickering who laid the ball back into the path of Ian Lawther and the forward hammered in a great shot from the edge of the area. From this moment on, there was only one team in it as Burnley were penned in their own half. The Clarets' desperate defence held out until the sixty-third minute when Rovers clinched the winner. Half-back Ronnie Clayton picked out Ian Lawther with a long ball down the middle that was squared to the far post where Fred Pickering rose high to beat Blacklaw with an oblique header that went in off the far post. It should have been three when a wonderful dribble by tricky Bryan Douglas took the winger past three defenders before slipping the ball to Eddie Thomas, who missed a glorious chance by hitting his shot straight at Blacklaw. Late in the game, Rovers nearly dropped a point when full-back Keith Newton miskicked a backpass that Towers intercepted and flashed in a cross, but no forward was able to get on the end of it.

By Easter, Burnley had booked their place in the FA Cup final and still led the title race before the fates decreed they would become the 'nearly men' of soccer history. The wheels came off their Championship challenge as they won only one of their last ten games. During this period, Rovers achieved their own

Tommy Cummings heads clear from Lawther, with (from left to right) Miller, Ratcliffe and Angus in close attendance.

remarkable 'double' when they visited Turf Moor and became the only team to beat the Clarets twice in the League. In the final analysis, these derby defeats were to cost Burnley dear. Honours might still have been theirs if they had won their last two League games, but a home defeat against bottom club Chelsea handed the title to First Division newcomers Ipswich Town. Assured of second spot, Burnley put out five reserves and lost their remaining League game at Sheffield United in a forlorn effort to rest key players before their Wembley date five days later. There was further heartbreak when holders Tottenham Hotspur retained the FA Cup and the promise of a momentous season fizzled out with Burnley being remembered for the cruellest 'double' of all – runners-up in the League and cup!

Blackburn Rovers (2-3-5)

Fred Else; Ken Taylor, Keith Newton; Ron Clayton, Matt Woods, Mick McGrath; Bryan Douglas, Ian Lawther, Fred Pickering, Eddie Thomas, Barrie Ratcliffe.
Manager: Jack Marshall.

Burnley (2-3-5)

Adam Blacklaw; John Angus, Alex Elder; Jimmy Adamson, Tommy Cummings, Brian Miller; John Connelly, Jimmy McIlroy, Ray Pointer, Jimmy Robson, Ian Towers.
Manager: Harry Potts.

FIRST DIVISION   1 JANUARY 1966

BLACKBURN ROVERS 0   BURNLEY 2

Attendance: 28,013

During the Summer, a serious polio epidemic had hit the town, resulting in several of Blackburn's early matches being postponed to prevent the spread of the killer disease. When Rovers' season finally got underway, the team won only one of their first ten games, before their fortunes appeared to have changed for the better when they gave Burnley a 4-1 hammering at Turf Moor. Alas, this was to be the highlight of the blue and whites' campaign. By the time the East Lancashire rivals met for the return, Blackburn were fighting for their First Division lives, while Burnley were pressing for the League Championship. With so much at stake for the clubs at different ends of the League spectrum, it was little wonder that this derby had extra spice and was played in an hostile atmosphere. The tensions resulted in a bad-tempered game and the dismissal of a player in the fixture for the first time since Blackburn's Jack Southworth and Burnley's Sandy Lang received their marching orders for fighting in 1892!

Burnley gained revenge for their home humiliation with a goal in each half which boosted their Championship hopes and plunged Rovers into deep relegation trouble. The opener came within twenty minutes. Brian O'Neil slipped a short free-kick to full-back Alex Elder, whose scorching drive was turned against the post by 'keeper Fred Else. Unluckily for the home side, the ball rebounded across the face of the goal where leading scorer Willie Irvine gratefully snapped up an easy chance. Three minutes earlier, Rovers had thrown away a golden opportunity to take the lead when Gordon Jones cleverly dribbled round the 'keeper into the six-yard box, then somehow contrived to shoot wide of an open goal.

Midway through the second period, Burnley's play-maker Gordon Harris collected a pass from Ralph Coates and sealed the match for the Clarets with a low skidding strike which gathered pace off the turf as it flew in from twenty-five yards. Desperation now crept into Blackburn's game and the tackles started flying. Up to this point, there had been far too many hold-ups for minor offences without any dirty play, but trouble erupted when Burnley were awarded free-kicks in quick succession for wild challenges on Harris committed by Dick Mulvaney and George Sharples. The Burnley wingers also came in for some rough treatment – Ralph Coates evaded an attempt to 'clog' him – then amused the away fans as he sat on the ball and invited the culprit to try again. His partner on the opposite flank, Scottish international Willie Morgan, reacted rather differently to the treatment and with eight minutes to go, was sent off following a flare-up with makeshift centre forward Mike England. The Welshman stayed on the field but was soon involved in another unsavoury incident with Adam Blacklaw. Aggravation spread to the terraces and the police became involved when a foolhardy spectator made a beeline for the

Defender Dick Mulvaney thwarts Willie Irvine with a sliding tackle.

Burnley 'keeper who held his attacker until the youth was escorted from the pitch.

Blackburn's woes continued and they finished the season well adrift at the foot of the division with only eight wins to their credit. Liverpool won the race for the League title and Burnley lost an opportunity of finishing runners-up. In their last home game of the season against Leeds United, a bizarre own goal, lobbed over the 'keeper from the acutest of angles by skipper Alex Elder, handed victory and second spot on goal average to their Yorkshire rivals!

Blackburn Rovers (2-3-5)

Fred Else; Keith Newton, Billy Wilson; Ron Clayton, Dick Mulvaney, George Sharples; Malcolm Darling, George Jones, Mike England, Mike Ferguson, Mike Harrison. Manager: Jack Marshall.

Burnley (2-3-5)

Adam Blacklaw; John Angus, Alex Elder; Brian O'Neil, Brian Miller, Sammy Todd; Willie Morgan, Arthur Bellamy, Willie Irvine, Gordon Harris, Ralph Coates. Manager: Harry Potts.

SECOND DIVISION   27 DECEMBER 1976
BLACKBURN ROVERS 2   BURNLEY 2
Attendance: 22,189

Burnley's relegation from the old First Division, only a year after Blackburn Rovers had climbed out of the Third Division, set up the first East Lancashire League derby for ten years. Tremendous entertainment was provided for Ewood Park's largest crowd of the season as they watched the first drawn game between the clubs in their tenth League meeting on the ground since the Second World War.

All the goals were scored in the second half of a match totally dominated by Rovers – until the visitors rallied to come back from two goals down and salvage a point in the last ten minutes. Burnley 'keeper Alan Stevenson was the busiest man on the field before half-time, making several fine saves to deny the Blackburn attack. The highlight of his display came with a breathtaking leap to tip a twenty-five-yard screamer from Stuart Metcalfe over the bar. Luck was on Burnley's side when the opposition skipper, Tony Parkes, missed a great chance, turning the ball wide of an open goal from close range; then John Byrom collected a pass from strike partner Bobby Svarc and was unfortunate to see his shot bounce out off a post.

The first half closed with Rovers ill-rewarded for their superiority, but after the resumption they took a well-deserved lead in the fifty-second minute, when a right-wing corner taken by Dave Wagstaffe was smartly converted at the near post by John Byrom. The same two players combined again for the second goal twelve minutes later when a free-kick was awarded just outside the penalty area. 'Waggy's' drive rebounded back to him off the defensive wall and he threaded the ball through for Byrom to force the ball home. With the home team now in effortless command, Burnley would probably have sunk without trace but for the brave Stevenson who made a daring dive at the feet of Bobby Svarc to prevent a goal which would have ended all hope of a recovery. After the two Byrom goals, Burnley boss Joe Brown pulled off Paul Fletcher and introduced winger Tony Morley, a shrewd move which permitted Peter Noble to move forward from midfield and give the attack some impetus. Equally, with fifteen minutes to go, their cause was helped by the decision of Rovers' manager Jim Smith to replace the injured Gordon Taylor by using substitute Neil Wilkinson in his normal position at right-back, moving Kevin Hird, who had performed brilliantly as an attacking defender, upfront to replace Taylor. These changes proved to be the turning point as Blackburn struggled to adjust to this new formation and Burnley gradually became more threatening. The arrears were reduced in the eightieth minute when defender Keith Newton's drive smacked against a post and Peter Noble snapped up the rebound to fire in off the underside of the bar. An equaliser which had seemed so unlikely, came with two minutes left. The referee incensed the home supporters by

Two-goal John Byrom.

ignoring a linesman's flag raised for offside, allowing Welsh international Brian Flynn to play on, before his cross reached Ian Brennan who hammered the ball into the net through a crowd of players. During a niggly second period the scorer was booked, along with teammate Billy Rodaway and Blackburn's Stuart Metcalfe, for over-zealous challenges, while Bryan Flynn and John Byrom were decidedly fortunate to remain on the field when the referee failed to spurt an off-the-ball flare-up in the last minute.

The Clarets won the rematch at Turf Moor but finished four places behind their local rivals in the bottom half of the division. Hopes of a return to the top flight were to remain on hold as both clubs were destined to leave the Second Division in the opposite direction!

Blackburn Rovers (4-3-3)
Paul Bradshaw; Kevin Hird, John Waddington, Terry Alcock, John Bailey; Stuart Metcalfe, Tony Parkes, Dave Wagstaffe; Bobby Svarc, John Byrom, Gordon Taylor (sub: Neil Wilkinson). Manager: Jim Smith.

Burnley (4-3-3)
Alan Stevenson; Keith Newton, Jim Thompson, Billy Rodaway, Ian Brennan; Brian Flynn, Peter Noble, Billy Ingham; Terry Cochrane, Malcolm Smith, Paul Fletcher (sub: Tony Morley). Manager: Joe Brown.

SECOND DIVISION   14 APRIL 1979
BLACKBURN ROVERS 1   BURNLEY 2
Attendance: 14,761

E wood Park was bathed in unseasonably strong sunshine and temperatures also soared on the terraces where police and ambulancemen were kept busy at the Darwen End. Violent scenes resulted in several people requiring treatment for injuries, while a few louts were ejected from the ground. Most East Lancashire supporters had come to watch the action on the field where Burnley, playing their fiftieth match of the season, completed an impressive League double over a Blackburn Rovers side decimated by injuries and haunted by the spectre of relegation.

Burnley looked dangerous from the start, when a Steve Kindon flick set Billy Ingham free, before he was intercepted by Tim Parkin who put the ball behind. From the corner, Joe Jakub hit a rising shot from twenty-five yards which cleared the bar. A slip by central defender John Waddington then let in Paul Fletcher, but the striker's shot flew well wide of the target. There was a bizarre incident after twenty minutes when a foul was awarded against Steve Kindon before he suddenly collapsed. The referee thought that the Burnley forward was 'making a meal of it' before realising that it was more serious. After receiving attention the player was stretchered off with a knee injury. Ten-man Burnley more than held their own before manager Harry Potts sent on substitute Tony Morley. Ironically, within a minute of returning to full strength, the visitors fell behind to a tremendous goal. Skipper John Bailey's cross was headed back to Simon Garner who gave 'keeper Alan Stevenson no chance with a thundering half-volley from the edge of the box. With new-found confidence, Rovers pressed forward and the charismatic Duncan McKenzie brought out a magnificent save from Stevenson, when he turned onto a ball and hammered it towards the top corner. Just before the interval, Blackburn 'keeper Neil Ramsbottom also distinguished himself, diving low to deny Paul Fletcher from point-blank range. A terrible defensive error ten seconds after the resumption gave the Clarets a shock equaliser. John Waddington intercepted a Leighton James cross, but was caught in possession by Tony Morley who took full advantage of the opportunity by cracking in a right-foot shot from the edge of the six-yard box. A minute later, the future England winger broke through again, only to see his shot shave the far post with Ramsbottom scrambling to cover. In the sixty-third minute, Rovers had a great chance to go in front when McKenzie crossed to Noel Brotherston, who completely miskicked while standing unmarked on the penalty spot. The home team were to regret this miss eight minutes later, when the visitors took the lead slightly against the run of play. Burnley's best move of the match began with Fletcher winning the ball in the air, ten yards inside Rovers' half on the left. Play quickly switched to the other flank where clever work by Tony Arins and

Leighton James congratulates Brian Hall upon netting the winner.

Tony Morley gave Peter Noble the chance to push the ball back into the path of Brian Hall who made no mistake, firing low and wide of the helpless Ramsbottom, for a worthy winner.

This result left Rovers in dire trouble at the bottom of the table and despite winning their last three games, they could not improve their position and were doomed to the Third Division. Despite their predicament the late rally won the hearts of the supporters, who even in the face of adversity, flocked onto the pitch after the last home game of the season to give their fallen heroes a rousing reception.

Blackburn Rovers (5-2-3)

Neil Ramsbottom; Mick Rathbone, Tim Parkin, John Waddington, Paul Round, John Bailey; Martin Fowler, Russell Coughlin; Noel Brotherston, Simon Garner, Duncan McKenzie. Manager: John Pickering.

Burnley (4-3-3)

Alan Stevenson; Tony Arins, Jim Thomson, Billy Rodaway, Joe Jakub; Brian Hall, Peter Noble, Billy Ingham; Paul Fletcher, Steve Kindon (sub: Tony Morley), Leighton James. Manager: Harry Potts.

SECOND DIVISION   4 APRIL 1983
BLACKBURN ROVERS 2   BURNLEY 1
Attendance: 13,434

In this pitiful Easter Derby, Blackburn Rovers at least emerged with the satisfaction of performing the 'double' and their first home League win over Burnley for twenty-one years. The result plunged the visitors deeper into the relegation mire and it was a black day for East Lancashire soccer with the unprecedented sight of a match at Ewood Park being held up for sixteen minutes in the second half. There were sickening scenes on the terraces as Burnley so-called 'supporters' went on the rampage in a pathetic attempt to get the game abandoned when their team fell behind.

On the field, the game was one of the worst in modern times between the old rivals, with little evidence of skill, flair or excitement. Within a minute, the home side's attacking options were severely curtailed when Ian Miller limped off with a knee injury. In a drastic reshuffle, substitute Norman Bell went up front, with Noel Brotherston switching to the right, leaving John Lowey on the left of midfield. The highlight of the first period occurred in the eleventh minute when Rovers should have taken the lead after 'keeper Alan Stevenson fumbled a Simon Garner cross, presenting David Hamilton with a gilt-edged opportunity which he lashed against the underside of the crossbar before the ball was cleared. Their only other real chance before the break was created when Bell was put clean through but shirked the responsibility by laying the ball off when there was no-one up in support. Burnley for their part, could only manage a half-hearted attempt from Kevin Young which flew well wide of the target. The deadlock was broken in the fifty-ninth minute when full-back Willie Donachie was harshly adjudged to have handled Brotherston's cross. Simon Garner sent the 'keeper the wrong way but was ordered to retake the penalty for encroachment by one of his teammates. The striker coolly replaced the ball on the spot and drove the ball into the same corner. Trouble, which had been brewing behind the Darwen End when a smoke-bomb was thrown onto the pitch, now escalated and Rovers' 'keeper Terry Gennoe became the target of a whisky bottle hurled from the crowd. The referee took the players off while order was restored by the police, assisted by Burnley manager Frank Casper who made a microphone appeal for calm. He later spoke to the press and disowned the unwanted faction who disgraced the club, branding them 'animals'.

Four minutes after the resumption, Rovers went two up through another controversial penalty. Hard-working David Hamilton darted through the middle and stumbled over from Brian Flynn's challenge as Stevenson dived at his feet to take the ball. This time, Garner required only one attempt to plant the spot kick in the net after seventy-six minutes. From the kick-off, Burnley created their first clear-cut chance when Steve Taylor's shot was well saved by Gennoe.

Simon Garner converted two penalties.

With five minutes of normal time remaining, the Clarets did reduce the arrears when a Martin Dobson free-kick was flicked on by Taylor for Derek Scott to stab home during a scramble from close range – but it came too late to influence the outcome.

Burnley won only two of their remaining ten matches and were consigned to the Third Division – from which they had been elevated as Champions at the end of the previous season. It was the parting of the ways for the East Lancashire clubs whose paths would not cross again in League action during the twentieth century.

Blackburn Rovers (4-5-1)
Terry Gennoe; Jim Branagan, David Mail, Derek Fazackerley, Mick Rathbone; Ian Miller (sub: Norman Bell), Colin Randell, David Hamilton, John Lowey, Noel Brotherston; Simon Garner. Manager: Bob Saxton.

Burnley (4-4-2)
Alan Stevenson; Brian Laws, Mike Phelan, Martin Dobson, Willie Donachie; Brian Flynn, Trevor Steven, Derek Scott, Kevin Young; Billy Hamilton, Steve Taylor. Manager: Brian Miller.

DIVISION ONE	17 DECEMBER 2000
BURNLEY 0	BLACKBURN ROVERS 2
Attendance: 21,369	

Although it had been seventeen long years since the East Lancashire rivals had met in meaningful League action, the years had obviously done little to ease the tensions between the two towns as this eagerly awaited derby was played-up for all it was worth in the pre-match media hype. In the intervening period, Blackburn had returned from their odyssey in the lower divisions to win the 1995 Premiership title before slipping out of the top flight again. In contrast, Burnley had sunk to the basement League and only secured their League survival in the very last game of a nail-biting season in 1987. Now both clubs were poised to return to the big time and this meeting would do much to illustrate which team was best prepared for the task.

Rovers bagged the points courtesy of goals by Jason McAteer and Marcus Bent in the dying seconds of each half. They took the lead after a defensive lapse by Burnley. Stig Bjornebye's long throw bounced over two defenders, but Paul Cook was in a good position to cover and clear the ball, yet he hesitated, allowing McAteer to hurl himself at the ball and bury his header under goalkeeper Nik Michopoulos. Rovers should have doubled their lead just after the break when Mark Hughes squandered a good opportunity, blazing over the bar from three yards out, after the ever-dangerous McAteer's shot had bobbled back off the post. Burnley could not capitalise on this good fortune and, urged on by their notoriously impatient supporters, abandoned their footballing beliefs in a desperate attempt to level the scores. The highly charged atmosphere was inflamed even more in the seventy-seventh minute when Kevin Ball sent David Dunn flying through the air with a ridiculous lunging challenge. As the referee waved the red card and Ball left the field, any chance that the Clarets had of salvaging something from the game went with him. They did find the net when John Mullin bundled the ball in following up an Andy Payton shot, but the effort was rightly disallowed for a foul on goalkeeper Brad Friedel. Any lingering doubts about the outcome were resolved shortly before the final whistle when substitute Matt Jansen drilled in a shot which the 'keeper could only knock up in the air and Rovers wrapped up the game through striker Marcus Bent, who had the simple task of nodding the ball into an unguarded net.

This vital result meant that Burnley had missed an opportunity to reach the top four and enabled Rovers to leapfrog over them into sixth position. For the rest of the season, the Clarets struggled to clinch a play-off place, while fast-improving Rovers secured automatic promotion. When the two teams met in the return at Ewood Park on 1 April, the home side made 'fools' of the Clarets, ably demonstrating the gap in class as they thrashed their opponents 5-0, the heaviest defeat that Burnley had suffered at the hands of their neighbours since

Marcus Bent wraps up
the game for Rovers.

1929. Despite making significant progress under manager Stan Ternent, this display exposed the Clarets as creditable over-achievers, for whom promotion would be a punishment, not a prize. In the event, Burnley just missed the play-offs, finishing seventh, making the club all the more determined to emulate neighbours Blackburn Rovers – preparing once more to savour the prospect of life in the Premiership.

Burnley (3-5-2)
Nik Michopoulos; Mitchell Thomas, Steve Davis, Ian Cox; Paul Cook (sub: Lenny Johnrose), Kevin Ball, Graham Branch (sub: Bradley Maylett), Micky Mellon (sub: John Mullin), Paul Weller; Andy Payton, Ian Moore. Manager: Stan Ternent.

Blackburn Rovers (4-4-2)
Brad Friedel; John Curtis, Henning Berg, Martin Taylor, Stig-Inge Bjornebye; Jason McAteer, Garry Flitcroft, David Dunn, Damien Duff (sub: Alan Mahon); Mark Hughes (sub: Matt Jansen), Marcus Bent. Manager: Graham Souness.

Burnley skipper Jimmy Adamson holds the League Championship trophy aloft after the club had pipped Wolves for the title in 1960. Coincidentally, the same two clubs share the dubious distinction of winning the Championship of all four divisions. The Clarets only other success in the top flight came under Tommy Boyle's leadership in 1921.

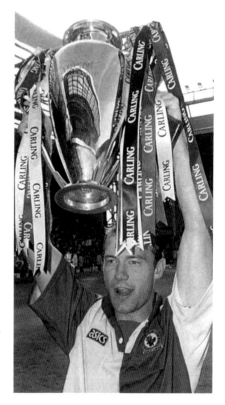

Alan Shearer played for Blackburn Rovers as they became Premier League Champions in 1995. The club had waited over eighty years to emulate the success of the team led by Bob Crompton which lifted the League Championship in 1912 and 1914.

5

DREAM TEAM – BURNLEY

Jimmy Adamson 1962. The only Burnley player to receive the Football Writer's Association 'Footballer of the Year' award is included in a fantasy squad of sixteen players to face the best of Blackburn Rovers in a 'Dream Derby'.

Jimmy Adamson
Centre-Back/Midfield
Born: Ashington, 4 April 1929

'The Man Who Won the World Cup' was how Jimmy Adamson jokingly described himself after his decision to turn down the England job – leaving the way clear for Alf Ramsey to lead the national side to an historic win in 1966. A one-club man who made almost 500 appearances for Burnley between 1950 and 1963, Jimmy filled all three traditional half-back positions but is best remembered for his role as defensive anchorman during a sparkling midfield partnership with Jimmy McIlroy. Captaining the side to the League Championship in 1960, Jimmy then became the only Claret to be awarded the Football Writers' award of Player of the Year in 1962 – the season he led the team to the FA Cup final. Playing for England 'B' in 1952 and selected as reserve for the senior international against Scotland the following year, Jimmy was described by Jimmy Greaves as 'the greatest player never to be capped by England', an opinion subscribed to by many astute soccer judges. Adamson's tactical acumen led to an appointment as England coach for the 1962 World Cup finals in Chile and he was also in the party as a player, but was not called upon by manager Walter Winterbottom, who resigned following the team's exit from the competition. Jimmy was the FA's choice as successor but he declined, owing to his lack of experience, and joined the Burnley coaching staff. Taking over as manager in 1970, he was haunted by a prophesy that Burnley would be 'the team of the Seventies' as they were immediately relegated in his first season at the helm. Returning to the top flight two years later, the club's need to sell their best players (Ralph Coates, Martin Dobson, Dave Thomas, Leighton James et al) hampered progress and Adamson's ambitions still remained unfulfilled when he parted company with the club in 1976. Having been associated with Burnley for thirty years serving as office boy, player, club captain, coach and manager, Jimmy is the ideal choice to take charge of the dream team.

Jerry Dawson
Goalkeeper
Born: Holme-in-Cliviger, nr Burnley,
   18 March 1887

In a career spanning over twenty years, Jerry Dawson established a club record of 522 appearances but will always be remembered for missing the biggest match in the club's history. A model of consistency and fitness throughout his career, he had the misfortune to be on the sidelines during Burnley's 1914 FA Cup triumph over Liverpool at Crystal Palace.

The village team goalkeeper was serving an apprenticeship with the Cliviger blacksmith when he came to the attention of Burnley scouts and signed professional forms shortly before his twentieth birthday in 1907. Jerry made his League debut that season and was to become a permanent fixture in the two great Burnley teams either side of the First World War. During his early days with the club, Burnley were struggling in the Second Division, but Jerry's fine displays gained international recognition when he was chosen to represent the Football League against the Scottish League at Ewood Park in 1910. Burnley slowly built a side capable of promotion which was achieved in 1913 and the following season carried off the FA Cup. Jerry picked up a thigh injury in the drawn semi-final against Sheffield United and reserve Ronnie Sewell proved a capable deputy in the replay. A week before the final, Jerry returned to first-team action hoping for a confidence-boosting game but received a further setback when his ribs were badly bruised as the Clarets crashed to a 4-1 defeat. Speculation was rife about his availability for the final, but Jerry made a selfless decision to stand down, worried he might not last the full ninety minutes. A special medal was struck for him in appreciation of his contribution to the club's success. Back between the posts after the First World War, Jerry was an integral part of the 1921 League Championship side. He was also awarded 2 long overdue England caps. On Christmas Day 1928, he made his final League bow. Aged forty, Jerry joined the coaching staff of the club he had served so well.

Colin Mcdonald

Goalkeeper

Born: Tottington, nr Bury, 15 October 1930

The sportswriters' choice as the best goalkeeper of the 1958 World Cup, Colin McDonald was generally regarded to be the greatest custodian to represent England since Frank Swift. Yet, at the pinnacle of his career, a tragic injury forced him into retirement just as Burnley assembled a team capable of winning top honours. Recommended to Burnley in 1948 by their full-back Jack Marshall (later manager of Blackburn Rovers), Colin had to wait six years for a first-team chance. Despite a heavy defeat at Aston Villa on his debut he established himself in the side and made the art of goalkeeping look deceptively easy with an unspectacular style which owed much to his uncanny anticipation and good positional sense. Recognition for his consistent displays came with a call-up to play for the Football League *v.* Scottish League in March 1958. A faultless performance earned him the first of 8 full caps, including four in the World Cup tournament held in Sweden where he particularly impressed in the goalless draw against the eventual champions Brazil. Only a year after winning his first representative honour, Colin collided with a forward and suffered a serious double-fracture of the leg while playing for the Football League *v.* League of Ireland. The following season, the Clarets won the League Championship while Colin struggled for fitness. Unable to recover full movement of the foot, he was compelled to accept that the 201st game he had played for the club would be his last. There would be few that would dispute Colin McDonald's right to rank alongside Jerry Dawson as Burnley's greatest-ever 'keeper. Had fate been kinder, there is little doubt that he would also have attained the legendary status accorded to England post-war greats Gordon Banks and Peter Shilton.

James Crabtree
Defender/Midfield
Born: Burnley, 23 December 1871

In 1895, Burnley created soccer history when they received the first-ever transfer fee in a deal with Aston Villa for local boy James Crabtree. The move came about through a contractual dispute in which the club refused to meet the international player's financial demands – dismissing them as 'exorbitant'. During five seasons at Turf Moor, James had proved himself to be a complete natural, capable of playing in goal and every outfield position, as well as captaining the side. His career with the Clarets ended after scoring 9 goals in 77 appearances, latterly at full-back where he was selected for three England games. During a golden period at Villa Park, he made a further eleven international appearances. Settling into the team at left-half, James made exactly 200 appearances in seven seasons for the Midlands giants, picking up three League Championship medals and an FA Cup winner's medal. In the 1897 final, James headed the winner in a 3-2 victory over Everton, which ensured that Villa emulated the achievement of Preston North End in becoming the second club to win the coveted League and cup double.

Tragically, behind this successful facade was an insecure individual with a strong over-reliance on alcohol which was to bring about a quick demise from a position as captain of his country. Released by Villa at the age of thirty, he briefly resurrected his League career at Plymouth Argyle before declining health, accelerated by his chronic drinking problem, brought on a series of fits which ended his life at the age of thirty-six.

George Halley

Defender
Born: Cronberry,
  29 October 1887

In March 1913, George Halley was signed from Bradford and was the final piece of the jigsaw which produced the historic half-back line of 'Halley, Boyle and Watson' on the Burnley team sheet. The trio were the backbone of the side during the club's glory years either side of the First World War. For a period, the Scotsman had to fight off considerable opposition for a place in the side from Levy Thorpe and often had to content himself with selection at left-back, before establishing himself in the team that carried off the FA Cup in 1914. The ageing half-back line reassembled after the First World War to surge to runners-up spot in 1920 and went one better the following season by carrying off the First Division title. During that momentous season, George received a belated call-up from the Scottish selectors for the international against Ireland, but was taken ill before the game and sadly, the thirty-three-year-old was never given another chance to represent his country. Having made twenty-six consecutive League appearances, he also missed the run-in to the League Championship. After one more campaign he turned down an offer to re-sign for the club and brought down the curtain on a wonderful career at Turf Moor where he made over 150 appearances for the Clarets in a half-back line remembered as one of the greatest of all time.

Tommy Boyle
Centre Half
Born: Hoyland, nr Barnsley,
   29 January 1888

Tommy Boyle leads out the Burnley team, closely followed by Billy Watson and George Halley.

In 1911, Burnley paid a club-record fee for Barnsley's Tommy Boyle who had captained the unfashionable Yorkshire club to the previous year's FA Cup final where they lost to Newcastle after a replay. The gritty Yorkshire pivot provided inspirational leadership qualities which helped motivate and transform the Clarets from a mediocre Second Division side to one of the best teams in the land either side of the First World War.

Despite measuring only 5' 7" tall, Tommy had phenomenal ability in the air, amply demonstrated when he out-jumped the defence to head the cup-tie decider against Rovers in 1913 (see match report, pages 38-39). The fulcrum of the legendary half-back line of Halley, Boyle and Watson which first graced Turf Moor as the team achieved promotion in 1913, Tommy was awarded his only international cap the following season when he also had the honour of becoming the first captain to receive the FA Cup from a reigning monarch when King George V witnessed Burnley's triumph over Liverpool at Crystal Palace. The club were on the verge of great things when war intervened and Bombadier Boyle received serious wounds while on active service in France, but recovered to take his place in the side which achieved a record unbeaten run of thirty matches to lift the League Championship in 1921. Now at the veteran stage, Tommy moved to Wrexham having contributed 43 goals in 236 matches for Burnley where he is still acknowledged as the club's best-ever leader.

Billy Watson
Defender
Born: Birkdale, Southport,
   11 September 1890

The youngest and longest-serving member of Burnley's immortal half-back line, left half Billy Watson was a one-club man who made 380 appearances for Burnley between 1909 and 1924. Once his silky skills had established him as an integral part of the first team, he became the most reliable and consistent player on the club's books for well over a decade. He won the first of 3 England caps against Scotland in March 1914 in an international career severely disrupted by the intervention of war.

The Halley, Boyle and Watson combination made their final appearance together against the old foe, Blackburn Rovers, in February 1922. No-one among the 40,000 crowd at Turf Moor realised they were witnessing the end of an era, for having lost by the odd goal in five at Ewood Park a week before, Burnley's chances of gaining revenge were dealt a severe blow when they were reduced to ten men midway through the first half. George Halley was stretchered off with torn ligaments as the home team lost 1-2. This was a sad way to end the half-back partnership which surprisingly had been limited to only 89 League and cup appearances together. Two-thirds of the line-up moved on at the end of the season, leaving Billy Watson as the only survivor. Retiring three years later, Billy later took a coaching role at Ewood Park and helped to develop youngsters by skippering the Rovers 'A' team in 1927.

Willie Morgan

Winger
Born: Glasgow, 2 October 1944

With his Beatles 'mop-top' hairstyle, Paul McCartney lookalike Willie Morgan symbolised the new breed of players in the 'Swinging Sixties' who attracted girls to football matches. He opened a Carnaby Street-style fashion boutique in Burnley and had an official fan club operating before fellow idol George Best!

When England winger John Connelly joined Manchester United in 1964, Burnley had a ready-made replacement in the skilful Scot with the crowd-pleasing style. In the post-League Championship period, his brilliance on the ball provided ample opportunities for the deadly twin strike force of Andy Lochhead and Willie Irvine. During the next four seasons the Clarets challenged without success for the top honours and despite winning 21 caps for Scotland and appearing at the 1974 World Cup finals, major prizes were to elude Willie throughout his career. In 1968, he trod the same path as his predecessor John Connelly, signing for reigning European Champions Manchester United who immediately added the World Club Championship to their trophy cabinet. Unfortunately, with the ensuing retirement of Matt Busby and George Best increasingly AWOL, the Reds went through a period of transition, eventually slipping out of the top flight for a season before bouncing back as Second Division Champions in 1975. The following season, Willie made a brief return to Turf Moor and brought his total up to 232 appearances for the club before giving sterling service to Bolton where he won another Second Division Championship medal. Spells with American clubs were followed by a final season of League action at Blackpool before Willie retired to pursue a career in public relations.

Jimmy McIlroy
Midfield
Born: Lambeg, 25 October 1931

'The Magic of McIlroy', 'Supermac' and 'the Irish leprechaun' were among the superlatives regularly attributed by sports journalists to applaud the genius of midfield maestro Jimmy McIlroy. Capped 55 times for Northern Ireland and a member of the Great Britain XI that faced the Rest of Europe in 1955, Jimmy scored over a century of goals in almost 500 appearances for Burnley after signing from Glentoran in 1950. His dazzling displays in an outstanding squad brought the League Championship to Burnley in 1960. Club chairman Bob Lord could not hide his disgust when his star was passed over for the 'Player of the Year' award in favour of Wolves captain Bill Slater. Jimmy was edged out again two years later, this time by Burnley skipper Jimmy Adamson who led the side to the FA Cup final at Wembley. There was constant conjecture about whether Jimmy might be a target for one of the glamour clubs but his sudden departure from Turf Moor in 1963 angered supporters and the reason is still shrouded in mystery. 'Mac' joined a Stanley Matthews-inspired Stoke City and helped restore the club to the First Division. Management roles with Stoke, Oldham and Bolton followed before he became a sports journalist in Burnley. Reporting on the Clarets' decline and fall to the Fourth Division was a sad assignment, although Jimmy responded to exasperated calls from fans to dust off his boots by wryly observing that even a twenty-five-year-old McIlroy could not halt the club's slide to the brink of non-League oblivion!

One of the 100 League Legends selected for the Football League's Hall of Fame in 1998, a further honour was bestowed in January 2000 when the Jimmy McIlroy stand was unveiled at Turf Moor as a lasting tribute to a worthy hero.

Opposite: An artist's impression of Jimmy McIlroy's career in April 1965.

"COMPETITION WITH CLUBS FROM OTHER COUNTRIES IS OBVIOUSLY THE PATTERN FOR THE FUTURE. I LEARNED SO MUCH FROM MY EUROPEAN CUP EXPERIENCE WITH BURNLEY."

JIMMY McILROY IS DEEP-THINKING AND KNOWLEDGEABLE, YET READY TO ADMIT HE IS STILL LEARNING.....

DARK, GOOD-LOOKING

HARRY POTTS, DEDICATED TO MAKING BURNLEY THE FINEST TEAM IN EUROPE, ADMITTED....

JIMMY IS SKILFUL, ARTISTIC — AN ABSOLUTE PERFECTIONIST.

...A FINE, FOOTBALLING INSIDE-FORWARD NOW WITH STOKE CITY, 'MAC' IS AN INSPIRATION TO YOUNGER PLAYERS.....

TURF MOOR REGULARS LOVED THE LITTLE IRISHMAN, NOT LEAST WHEN HIS PENALTY KICKS SENT GOALIES TUMBLING IN THE WRONG DIRECTION......

...IN 1960 BURNLEY WERE WORTHY LEAGUE CHAMPIONS, THUS QUALIFYING FOR THE EUROPEAN CUP COMPETITION THE FOLLOWING SEASON. SAID CHAIRMAN BOB LORD...

McILROY WAS BEHIND THAT TITLE WIN — BRILLIANT IN EVERY GAME. THE FOOTBALL WRITERS HAD THE NERVE TO PICK SOMEONE ELSE AS 'FOOTBALLER OF THE YEAR', OF COURSE, I STOOD UP AT THE DINNER AND TOLD THEM WHAT I THOUGHT OF BILL SLATER, THEIR CHOICE —— AND HE WAS SITTING NEXT TO ME!

AFTER KNOCKING OUT RHEIMS IN THE FIRST ROUND, BURNLEY WON THE FIRST LEG OF THEIR SECOND ROUND TIE WITH HAMBURG BY 3-1 AT TURF MOOR..

NEVERTHELESS THE MAGNIFICENT GERMAN CENTRE-FORWARD UWE SEELER PROVED TOO STRONG FOR GALLANT BURNLEY IN HAMBURG, AND OUT THEY WENT BY THE ODD GOAL.....

....BUT WHAT IF McILROY'S LAST MINUTE SHOT HAD GONE IN, INSTEAD OF HITTING A POST?

HAMBURG'S WIN DID BURNLEY LESS THAN JUSTICE, BUT THAT'S FOOTBALL..ENGLISH TEAMS THINK THEY ARE GOOD UNTIL THEY MEET THE CREAM OF EUROPE. UNLESS YOU'VE TAKEN PART, YOU'VE NO IDEA.......

IN THE 1962 CUP-FINAL 'SPURS' SHOULDERS DROOPED WHEN ROBSON EQUALISED FOR BURNLEY—ONLY TO BE LIFTED A MINUTE LATER AS BOBBY SMITH PICKED UP A SOFT GOAL! AS IN THE LEAGUE THE TURF MOOR BOYS HAD TO BE CONTENT TO BE 'RUNNERS-UP.'

McILROY DIDN'T MISS A HOME INTERNATIONAL FOR IRELAND BETWEEN 1962 AND 1960, HIS GREATEST MOMENT COMING WHEN HELPING THEM TO A SPLENDID 3-2 WIN AT WEMBLEY IN 1957......

...IT CAME AS A SHOCK WHEN BURNLEY PUT JIMMY ON THE TRANSFER LIST, BUT SECOND DIVISION STOKE, ALREADY WITH MATTHEWS, MUDIE AND VIOLLET IN THEIR SIDE, WEREN'T SLOW TO SNAP HIM UP.....

HE HELPED CITY TO PROMOTION THE SAME SEASON (1963) AND POTTERY FANS HOPE HE WILL STILL TORMENT FIRST DIVISION DEFENCES FOR YEARS TO COME.

R. BOND '65

117

Martin Dobson
Centre-Back/Midfield
Born: Rishton,
 14 February 1948

Martin Dobson pictured with protégé Lee Dixon.

An elegant and stylish footballer whose intelligent probing from midfield won him 5 England caps, Martin Dobson captained the Burnley side in two promotion seasons as the club vainly tried to regain the glory days of the early 1960s. Converted from centre forward, where he made his debut for the club in 1967, Martin oozed class in a side that slipped out of the top flight. Leading the club to the Championship of the Second Division in 1973, Everton paid a British-record transfer fee a year later to prise him away to Goodison Park where he spent five seasons and became an integral part of the Blues' side which narrowly failed to land any of the major honours. In 1979, he returned to Turf Moor and immediately the club were consigned to life in the Third Division. Two years later, Martin captained the side to the Third Division Championship, but hopes of a revival were quickly dashed as they slid straight down again. After making almost 500 appearances for the Clarets, Martin moved to Bury in 1984, later managing the club with former Clarets Ray Pointer and Frank Casper on the coaching staff. This was the first step of a long career with various clubs on the non-playing side of the game. Under Martin's management, the Shakers won promotion from the Fourth Division. An inspired signing for the club was former Burnley teammate Lee Dixon, who had joined Chester after being freed by manager John Bond. The full-back resurrected his career at Gigg Lane and moved on to Stoke City before winning club and international honours with Arsenal.

Bob Kelly
Midfield
Born: Ashton-in-Makerfield,
   16 November 1893/4

A creative genius whose vision and superb ball control, allied to skilful distribution and an eye for goal, made him one of the greatest players to wear the claret and blue. Signed from St Helen's Town in 1913, Bob did not win a place in the Clarets' FA Cup-winning team a year later, but when League soccer resumed after the First World War he reached his peak, scoring 20 goals in 37 appearances as Burnley lifted the League Championship in 1921. His form the previous season had brought him to the notice of the England selectors and he won the first of 14 caps, scoring twice on his debut in the 5-4 defeat of Scotland. Needing only one more game to accomplish 300 appearances for the Clarets, supporters were stunned by the club's decision to sell him to Sunderland in December 1925. Perhaps the management thought a British-record fee for a thirty-one-year-old player was good business, but Bob proved he was still a force to be reckoned with eighteen months later, when he left Wearside to join Huddersfield Town. He was to make over 200 appearances for the Terriers and in 1927/28 the club narrowly failed to achieve the 'double', finishing runners-up to Everton in the League and losing to Blackburn Rovers in the FA Cup final. Bob received another FA Cup losers' medal two years later when Huddersfield were defeated by Arsenal – managed by Town's former manager Herbert Chapman.

Tommy Lawton

Striker

Born: Bolton, 6 October 1919

In an all-too-brief stay at Turf Moor, Burnley's greatest-ever discovery made his first-team debut as a sixteen-year-old amateur and in his first match as a professional gave England centre half Arthur Rowley a torrid time by scoring a hat-trick against Spurs. On the first step of a brilliant career that would produce 22 goals in 23 games for England, Tommy never forgot the invaluable coaching he had received at Turf Moor from former Welsh international Ray Bennion, nor the sound advice he received from a teammate after notching his first League goals at Swansea: 'Don't think too much of thyself. Tha've a long way to go and a lot to learn.' The teenage sensation scored 16 goals in 25 matches before attracting the bigger clubs and Burnley, languishing in the Second Division, could not afford to turn down an offer from Everton. On Merseyside, Tommy was undaunted, playing alongside and later emulating the immortal Dixie Dean. The club won the First Division Championship in 1939 and after the Second World War Tommy moved to Chelsea for one season. In 1947, Third Division Notts County shocked the soccer world by smashing the transfer record to sign the charismatic crowd-puller. Their boldness was rewarded when gates were tripled as Tommy's 31 goals won them promotion. After a spell at Brentford, the thirty-five-year-old was recalled to the top flight for a glorious swansong with Arsenal before bowing out three years later to manage non-League Kettering Town.

A Rolls-Royce among strikers with all-round skill and lethal two-footed finishing, Tommy's outstanding ability was in the air, made possible by a spectacular hovering leap and perfect timing. He set the standard for modern-day centre forwards and Alan Shearer's emergence as a world-class striker at Ewood Park earned him favourable comparisons with the maestro of old.

Opposite: A pictorial account of Tommy Lawton's rise to fame.

TOMMY LAWTON FIRST APPEARED FOR BURNLEY AT CENTRE-FORWARD JUST FOUR DAYS AFTER HIS SEVENTEENTH BIRTHDAY, AGAINST 'SPURS. BEFORE THE END OF THE MATCH THE CHEERS AND THE HANDSHAKES ANNOUNCED THAT HE HAD MARKED HIS DEBUT WITH A FINE HAT-TRICK...

NOT LONG AFTERWARDS EVERTON PAID BURNLEY £6,500 FOR THE BOY, SEEING HIM AS SUCCESSOR TO DIXIE DEAN. SURE ENOUGH, IN 1939 THE 'BLUES' WON THE LEAGUE CHAMPIONSHIP, LAWTON CONTRIBUTING 35 GOALS.

THOUGH NOT QUITE SO SPECTACULAR AS DEAN, LAWTON LED THE ATTACK IN THE SAME STYLE, HEADING AND SHOOTING GOALS WITH SIMILAR POWER.

TOMMY'S INTERNATIONAL CAREER HAD BEGUN THAT SAME SEASON, AND HIS FIRST GAME AGAINST SCOTLAND AT HAMPDEN WAS A THRILLER. IN THE LAST MINUTE HE HEADED A SENSATIONAL WINNING GOAL FOR ENGLAND FROM A PERFECT CROSS BY MATTHEWS, AND HIS DELIGHTED COLLEAGUES MOBBED HIM LIKE A BUNCH OF SCHOOLKIDS...

HIS ABILITY TO CLIMB TO A HIGH CENTRE, HEAD AND SHOULDERS ABOVE HIS OPPONENTS, AND DRIVE THE BALL INTO THE GOAL WITH HIS SHINING BLACK HEAD AND STRONG NECK MUSCLES WAS ONE OF THE UNFORGETTABLE SIGHTS IN SOCCER.

AFTER TEN HAPPY YEARS AT GOODISON, LAWTON WAS BOUGHT BY CHELSEA IN 1945 FOR A RECORD £11,500.

IN THAT NEVER-TO-BE-FORGOTTEN GOAL RUSH IN PORTUGAL IN 1947 LAWTON HAMMERED IN FOUR OF ENGLAND'S TEN GOALS....

THE TREMENDOUS POWER IN HIS LEGS GAVE HIM THIS SPRING, AND ALSO A QUICKNESS OFF THE MARK AND A LETHAL SHOT IN EACH FOOT.

LAWTON'S SCORED AGAIN!

IN THE BIG GAME AGAINST THE FAMOUS MOSCOW DYNAMOS HE HEADED ANOTHER SPECTACULAR GOAL IN A 3-3 DRAW, AND HIS 26 GOALS IN THAT FIRST SEASON AT STAMFORD BRIDGE WAS AGAIN A RECORD.

R. BOND

WHETHER ON THE GREAT STADIUMS OF EUROPE OR ON MUDDY THIRD DIVISION PITCHES HE WAS STILL THE MASTER. HE WOULD PROWL WATCHFULLY AND POUNCE WITH DEADLY SPEED ON ANY OPPORTUNITY MADE FOR HIM. EVERYTHING ABOUT HIM WAS A THREAT, YET HE NEVER LOST HIS TEMPER. ENGLAND HAS HAD FEW, IF ANY, LIKE TOMMY LAWTON.

HE MOVED AROUND FROM CHELSEA TO NOTTS COUNTY AND THEN BRENTFORD. IN 1953 ARSENAL, STRUGGLING NEAR THE FOOT OF DIVISION ONE, ASTONISHED THE FOOTBALL WORLD BY SIGNING 34-YEAR-OLD LAWTON. HE SCORED FEW GOALS, BUT HIS STEADYING INFLUENCE LIFTED THE GUNNERS OUT OF TROUBLE. AFTER THREE SEASONS AT HIGHBURY, TOMMY HUNG UP HIS BOOTS FOR THE LAST TIME.

Leighton James
Winger
Born: Llwchwyr,
    16 February 1953

Skill, pace and spectacular shooting ability marked Leighton James out as something special even by Burnley's high standards. Capped 54 times by Wales, he made some 400 appearances for the Clarets in three spells with the club between 1971 and 1989. He was also a volatile character on the pitch with an edge to his game that mild-mannered England international Trevor Brooking summed up from personal experience: 'Leighton gnawed away at the opposition like a toothache and I should think quite a number of players were cautioned for retaliatory tackles made against him.'

Making his debut in 1971 during Burnley's relegation season, Leighton was an ever-present two seasons later when the Clarets returned to the top flight as champions of the Second Division. Established as another brilliant success of the club's scouting and coaching scheme, the next stage was a familiar one to Burnley fans, Leighton was sold to balance the books and it was Derby who came in with a club-record offer to tempt him away. His playing days with the Rams and later QPR did not quite match up to his best days at Burnley and in 1978, he returned to the fold in time to take part in the Anglo-Scots Cup win. Leaving for Swansea two years later when the Clarets slipped into the Third Division for the first time in their history, Leighton played his part in elevating the Swans to the top flight and a place in Europe, then had spells with Sunderland, Bury and Newport before taking up a player-coach role at Turf Moor during the League survival crisis of 1987 when the club pulled off The Great Escape. A walk-on part as substitute in the 1988 Sherpa Van Trophy final at Wembley was a fitting return to the big stage for a player whose twenty-year career had run parallel to Burnley's fall from the First to the Fourth Division.

Ray Pointer
Striker
Born: Shankhouse, 10 October 1936

The 'Blonde Bombshell' of Burnley's title-winning side in 1960, Ray Pointer had a phenomenal work rate for a striker. A tireless runner who never gave defenders a moment's peace, a favourite ploy was to drag markers out of position by making decoy runs along the flanks, thereby creating openings for his colleagues. Despite this all-action selfless style Ray averaged a goal every two games for the Clarets and became the club's most prolific post-war scorer with 133 goals in 270 games.

Signing for Burnley after completing National Service in 1957, Ray quickly established himself in the side which within three years had lifted the League title. In his first full season he set a post-war record of 27 League goals. During a golden period for the club when they lifted the League title and reached the final of the FA Cup, Ray also collected 3 England caps and he and club colleague John Connelly scored in the 2-0 win over Portugal which ensured England's qualification for the 1962 World Cup in Chile. Ray was not included in the party and the next season he suffered a serious ankle injury which required surgery. Recovery seemed complete and he was soon back on the goal mark for the reserve team, but with Andy Lochhead and Willie Irvine settling as a formidable strike force, Ray found himself on the sidelines and in 1965 he moved to Bury. At Gigg Lane, 17 goals in 19 outings attracted the attention of ambitious manager Jimmy Hill who signed him for Coventry where he notched 13 goals in 23 games before a final move to Portsmouth where he served for six years, converting to a midfield role. Various coaching posts followed including a welcome return to Turf Moor where he was appointed youth team manager in 1978.

Ewood Park 7 March 1959. Ray Pointer in a mid-air clash with marker Matt Woods.

Willie Irvine
Striker
Born: Carrickfergus, East Antrim,
   18 June 1943

Willie Irvine's earliest opportunity to play alongside club colleagues Jimmy McIlroy and Alex Elder came when he was awarded the first of 23 caps for Northen Ireland in 1963. International recognition came before he had broken through into the League team at Burnley which had enjoyed great success with an attack led by post-war scoring-record holder Ray Pointer. Once established in the side, Willie's prolific feats in front of goal enabled him to overhaul the England centre forward's total with 29 League goals in season 1965/66. The striker's 37 goals in all competitions also bettered the feats of pre-war Claret legends Bert Freeman and George Beel.

Despite scoring six hat-tricks and amassing an incredible ratio of 97 goals in only 148 games, Willie's record-breaking exploits in the top flight suffered a serious setback when he broke a leg during a FA Cup-tie in January 1967. During the match with Everton, he had notched his 14th goal in his 24th start of the season. Once recovered he was never able to recapture the same level of performance that had highlighted him as a marksman of the highest calibre. In 1968, he was allowed to move on, gradually slipping down the divisions with Preston, Brighton and Halifax. Had fate not dealt such a cruel hand, it is certain that the ace goal poacher would have seriously challenged Ray Pointer's other post-war record of 133 goals for Burnley. In the event, the two individual records Willie set remained safely out of reach for the remainder of the twentieth century.

Opposite Page

Above: Willie Irvine's ambition was clear as he closed in on Burnley's post-war scoring record in May 1966.

Below: Willie snaps up one of the 29 record-breaking League goals at Ewood Park as Burnley beat Blackburn Rovers 2-0 on New Year's Day 1966.

WILLIE IRVINE HAS HIS EYE ON...

...THAT BURNLEY RECORD

Belfast last winter, and a dramatic overhead kick gives Willie, and Ireland, the winning goal against Scotland.

❝ I want to top Ray Pointer's 27 goals in a season ❞

Trevor Steven
Midfield
Born: Berwick-upon-Tweed, 21 September 1963

The last great product of Burnley's post-war youth policy which floundered as the club descended to the depths of the Football League, seventeen-year-old Trevor Steven made his debut for the Clarets in 1981 and was earmarked as a future international when he emerged as the star of the side which were promoted as Third Division Champions. The following season, the club enjoyed good cup runs in the League Cup and FA Cup but their form in the League was abysmal and they slid straight out of the Second Division. Having completed a century of appearances for the club, it came as no surprise when a £325,000 offer from Everton was accepted for the brilliant midfielder in July 1983. At Goodison Park, Trevor was a key member of the side which swept all before them in the mid-1980s, collecting two League Championships and winners' medals in the FA Cup and European Cup Winner's Cup. During this period, Trevor was also awarded the first of 36 England caps and played in the 1984 World Cup team eliminated in the quarter final by Argentina and divine intervention from Maradona's 'Hand of God'. In June 1989, Trevor moved to Glasgow Rangers who were then enjoying a reign of supremacy over their bitter rivals Celtic. After picking up a Scottish League Cup winners' medal and two Scottish Premier League Championships, Trevor joined Marseilles for £5.5M and added the French Championship to his growing list of honours before returning to Ibrox in 1992. The Scottish giants comfortably held on to the Championship for a further four seasons before Trevor brought the curtain down on a glittering career as the most highly decorated ex-Claret.

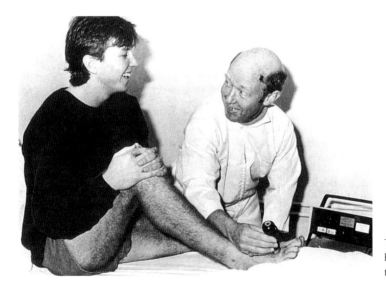

Trevor Steven smiles bravely on the treatment table at Turf Moor.

Burnley Dream Team

Colin McDonald

George Halley   Tommy Boyle   Billy Watson

Jimmy McIlroy   Martin Dobson   Bob Kelly

Willie Morgan   Leighton James

Tommy Lawton   Ray Pointer

Subs: Jerry Dawson, James Crabtree, Jimmy Adamson, Trevor Steven, Willie Irvine.

The starting line-up for the Burnley 'dream team' has an attacking formation with the holy trinity of Halley, Boyle and Watson providing a formidable barrier in front of one of England's finest post-war goalkeepers Colin McDonald. When necessary, central-midfield lynchpin Martin Dobson can slip alongside skipper Boyle to bolster the defence. Creativity will be supplied in abundance by the marvellous midfield pairing of the two greatest players to don the claret and blue – Bob Kelly and Jimmy McIlroy. Wide-men Willie Morgan and Leighton James can backtrack to cover danger down the flanks and will pose a threat through their ability to take on defenders and supply accurate crosses for the prolific goalscoring talents of Tommy Lawton and Ray Pointer. Player-manager Jimmy Adamson can make tactical variations where necessary with four brilliant internationals alongside him on the subs bench itching to get into the action: goalkeeper Jerry Dawson, defender James Crabtree, midfield dynamo Trevor Steven and striker Willie Irvine. Utilising the fine tradition of the rugby-playing Barbarians, the team kicks-off including one previously uncapped footballer in George Halley.

The immortal Halley, Boyle and Watson form the backbone of the fantasy line-up.

Burnley Dream Team

Colin McDonald

George Halley   Tommy Boyle   Billy Watson

Jimmy McIlroy   Martin Dobson   Bob Kelly

Willie Morgan   Tommy Lawton   Ray Pointer   Leighton James

6

DREAM TEAM – BLACKBURN ROVERS

Alan Shearer became the first Blackburn Rovers player to receive the prestigious Footballer of the Year award in 1994. He leads the attack in the following selection of great players who form the fantasy squad to face Burnley in the ultimate Dream Derby.

Bob Crompton
Defender
Born: Blackburn,
   26 September 1879

Defender Bob Crompton set the standard by which all Blackburn Rovers players are judged and he still remains the greatest name in the proud history of the club. A national figure who elevated the status of professional soccer by becoming the first non-amateur captain of England, he also had the distinction of being the first professional able to afford to drive his own car to a football match!

Bob made the first of 608 appearances for his hometown club in 1897. Initially a centre half, he was converted to full-back on the left flank before switching to the right where he was to become an automatic choice for his country, winning a record 41 caps between 1902 and the outbreak of war in 1914. In the meantime, he led Rovers to two League Championship successes in 1912 and 1914. He retired after making two post-war appearances in 1920 and his greatest regret was that he never led the club to an FA Cup final, thereby emulating the feats of previous Rovers teams that had won the trophy five times before his career had begun. Ironically, the honour that had eluded him as a player was secured while he was honorary manager of the club in 1928. A second spell at the helm restored Blackburn to the First Division before the outbreak of war in 1939. His last game in charge was a 3-2 wartime home win over old rivals Burnley. Later that evening in March 1941, soccer's first superstar tragically collapsed and died leaving a void at Ewood Park that could never been adequately filled. Having played such a great part in bringing success to Ewood Park on and off the field, Bob is the natural choice to take charge of the fantasy squad.

Herbie Arthur
Goalkeeper
Born: Blackburn, 14 February 1863

Joining Blackburn Rovers as a wing half in 1880, Herbie Arthur had hidden talents that were discovered two years later when he volunteered to keep goal for the reserves when they were a man short. Onlookers realised he was a natural with an unspectacular style built on a sound positional sense. Selected for England on seven occasions, he had the distinction of becoming the club's first custodian to represent the national side and presented a formidable barrier for Rovers in the mid-1880s when they carried off the FA Cup three times.

When the Football League was formed in 1888, Herbie picked up a serious knee injury midway through the season and subsequently left Ewood Park to play non-League soccer. Injuries to two goalkeepers on the books persuaded him to return in 1891 on the understanding that he would be allowed to captain the team. In December that year, he took part in the most bizarre derby of them all when the League game against Burnley was played in a severe blizzard at Turf Moor. Trailing 3-0 at half-time and with the weather worsening, only seven Blackburn players took the field for the second half. Matters got worse a few minutes after the restart when a fight between Burnley skipper Alex Stewart and Blackburn winger Joe Lofthouse resulted in them both receiving their marching orders. The remaining Blackburn outfield players also declined to continue, leaving Herbie Arthur to face the home side alone! The referee restarted the match and the 'keeper successfully appealed for offside but with no-one to pass to, he delayed taking the free-kick and the whistle sounded to abandon the ludicrous affair!

Fred Else
Goalkeeper
Born: Golborne, 31 March 1933

Readers of a national newspaper voted Fred Else 'England's best uncapped goalkeeper' while he was at Preston North End. He was unlucky not to add to England 'B' honours as his calm, authoritative displays made him an automatic choice for seven seasons as he made over 200 appearances for the club during the era of the great Tom Finney. Firmly established as one of the country's top goalkeepers, Fred became unsettled at Deepdale following the lifting of the maximum wage in 1961. This led to a contractual dispute with the club who did not meet his valuation and he unexpectedly became available for transfer. Fred was immediately snapped up by Blackburn Rovers and within a few hours of making the short journey to Ewood Park to agree terms, played his first game for Rovers in a pre-season evening friendly against his former Preston teammates!

First-choice 'keeper for five seasons, Fred's assured reading of the game and safe handling was a soccer connoisseur's delight as he made 221 League and Cup appearances for Rovers. He suffered a setback in February 1965 when he broke a collarbone in a League derby against Burnley. Once recovered, the following season was disastrous for Rovers when they plunged out of the top flight. As the club sought to rebuild a team capable of regaining former glories, Fred was released and signed for Fourth Division Barrow. As always, he gave sterling service making 148 appearances and briefly managing the club before they failed to win re-election to the Football League in 1972.

Ewood Park, 19 October 1963. Even Fred Else is powerless to stop this shot from Burnley's John Connelly.

Jimmy Forrest
Midfield
Born: Blackburn, 24 June 1864

A slightly-built, intelligent playmaker, wing half Jimmy Forrest represented England on eleven occasions and was the only Rovers' player to participate in the club's glorious run of five FA Cup final wins achieved between 1884 and 1891. The *Lancashire Evening Express* summed up their admiration for Jimmy's ability: 'In his own position, Forrest when in his best form, has no superiors, and few equals. His tackling is most determined, and the judgement with which he feeds his forwards is almost faultless.'

When professionalism was officially recognised in 1885, Jimmy joined the paid ranks and the following season became the first professional to play for England. Their opponents Scotland protested that both teams should be strictly amateur and when the game was eventually allowed to go ahead, Jimmy was made to wear a tighter shirt than his colleagues to distinguish him from the 'gentlemen'. Shortly before Blackburn's fifth FA Cup success in 1891, Jimmy gave up his job in a cotton mill to become a pub landlord. He left Rovers to play for Darwen four years later, following a dispute with the committee, which was later forgiven and forgotten when he returned to serve as a director of the club for which he had made 195 League and cup appearances.

Harry Healless
Defender
Born: Blackburn,
  10 February 1893

Wembley, FA Cup final 1928. Harry Healless (left) shakes hands with Huddersfield skipper Clem Stephenson.

Not the most naturally gifted of footballers, Harry Healless made it to the top by sheer grit and determination. The hardworking half-back initially arrived at Ewood Park as an inside forward just before the outbreak of the First World War. He was twenty-six years old before he made his League debut in 1919 and it took him a further two seasons to establish himself as a regular in the side. Gradually, his qualities were recognised as he won the first of 2 England caps in 1925. The second was awarded three years later, a month before he captained his hometown club to FA Cup success at Wembley. The 1928 FA Cup win was a major shock against double-chasing Huddersfield, whose star-studded team included former Burnley great Bob Kelly. Now at the veteran stage, Harry played on until he was forty and required only one more game to notch up 400 appearances for Rovers when he retired. Given a backroom role at Ewood Park, Harry left to coach a Dutch club in 1935. Upon his return to Lancashire, he showed he had not lost his love of playing and in 1948 at the age of fifty-five, he was partnering his son at full-back in a local League side. When the call came from Ewood Park in 1951, he undertook the role of club coach and the signs looked good as Rovers embarked on a thrilling FA Cup run, defeating Burnley in the sixth round before falling to eventual winners Newcastle United in a semi-final replay. Forever loyal to the club he had served on and off for forty years, Harry stepped down without a murmur of complaint when Johnny Carey was appointed manager in 1953.

Bill Eckersley
Defender
Born: Southport,
   16 July 1925

One of Rovers' finest defenders was discovered in unusual circumstances when Blackburn 'A' team's opponents Feniscowles were a man short and Bill Eckersley stepped in to play in borrowed boots laced up with string. The slightly-built tenacious full-back immediately impressed and made his League debut as the blue and whites were heading for relegation in 1948. Only two years later he became Alf Ramsey's full-back partner in the England side and made 17 appearances in trying times for the national side. Awarded his first cap against Spain in the opening round of the 1950 World Cup, Bill was omitted from the side which was humiliated by the USA and played his last international in the team outclassed at Wembley by Hungary in 1953. Although never recalled to the international scene, his club form as captain of Blackburn was exceptional as the club challenged to win a spot back in the top flight. This was achieved in 1958, but injury problems restricted Bill's future participation to a handful of games and he missed the cup run to Wembley in 1960. Having made 407 appearances for Rovers he retired the following season and 21,000 supporters turned out at his testimonial to pay tribute to one of Ewood Park's favourite sons. Following Bill's premature death at the age of fifty-four, his ashes were scattered on the ground he had graced for so long.

Ronnie Clayton
Central Defender/Midfield
Born: Preston, 5 August 1934

Given his first taste of senior soccer in a 'friendly' against Burnley in 1951, sixteen-year-old Ronnie Clayton took the first tentative step along a career that would set a then-club record of 665 League and cup appearances. A year later, he was a member of the Rovers team that reached the FA Cup semi-final, before National Service interrupted his progress. Returning to civvy street, he formed an impressive half-back partnership with his elder brother Ken, whose career was ended prematurely by a broken leg in 1957. The following season, Ronnie was the driving force behind Rovers' successful promotion campaign as he skippered the side back to the First Division. Ronnie gained his first England cap in 1955 and was seen as the natural successor to Billy Wright who retired as captain of the national side in 1959. Given an opportunity to impress by leading the Football League against the League of Ireland, the game was overshadowed by a career-ending injury to Burnley goalkeeper Colin McDonald. Although Ronnie subsequently led the England team in five internationals, his ambition to beat the club record of 43 caps awarded to Bob Crompton was never realised. A few weeks after leading out Blackburn in the 1960 FA Cup final against Wolves, Ronnie played his 35th and last international and was then dropped in favour of future England manager Bobby Robson.

Although never regaining the favour of the England selectors, Ronnie's strong-tackling forceful style continued to serve his club well. Towards the end of his playing days, when the characteristic surges from midfield became more arduous, his defensive capabilities and ability in the air enabled him to adapt to a role in the middle of the back four. Following his retirement in 1969, Ronnie received a long-service award from the Football League in recognition of his twenty years of loyalty to Blackburn Rovers.

Opposite: Ron Clayton's career illustrated in October 1965.

"WHETHER YOU'RE A GROUND STAFF LAD JUST STARTING AT THE BOTTOM OR A WELL-ESTABLISHED STAR, YOU MUST PUT 100 PER CENT INTO ALL YOU DO. YOU MUST BE FOOTBALL-DAFT." BLACKBURN AND ENGLAND WING-HALF RONNIE CLAYTON'S SUCCESS HAS BEEN FOUNDED ON HARD WORK, CONSTANT PRACTICE AND A PASSION FOR PHYSICAL FITNESS.

CLAYTON'S HOME TOWN CLUB, PRESTON CONSIDERED HIM TOO SMALL. BUT BLACKBURN'S MANAGER JACKIE BESTALL LIKED WHAT HE SAW....

IF THIS YOUNGSTER DOESN'T PLAY FOR ENGLAND ONE DAY THEN EITHER I'M A DUTCHMAN OR HE IS.

ROVERS WERE PERILOUSLY CLOSE TO BEING RELEGATED TO DIVISION THREE WHEN RONNIE FIRST BEGAN TO MAKE HIS IMPACT AT RIGHT HALF IN 1952.....

SPORT HOLDERS THROUGH MITCHELL WINS

FOOTBALL: LATE PENALTY BEATS UNLUCKY BLACKBURN 17-YEAR-OLD CLAYTON PLAYS TIRELESSLY

NATIONAL SERVICE DELAYED THE DEVELOPMENT OF CLAYTON'S CAREER, BUT NEVERTHELESS HE SOON RECOVERED HIS PROMISE AND IN 1955 WON HIS FIRST CAP.....

BUT DESPITE THEIR PRECARIOUS LEAGUE POSITION THEY MADE A BRAVE ATTEMPT TO LIFT THE CUP, TAKING THE ULTIMATE WINNERS, NEWCASTLE, TO A SEMI-FINAL REPLAY....

THESE GAMES ARE TWO OF MY MOST STIRRING MEMORIES. BUT WHEN I WAS CALLED INTO THE SERVICES I HAD RATHER TOO MUCH FOOTBALL. IT KEPT ME VERY FIT, BUT IT DIDN'T DO MUCH ELSE. I SOON BEGAN TO WISH IT WAS OVER....

RONNIE HELPED ENGLAND TO BEAT IRELAND 3-0 AND SPAIN 4-1....

"ANOTHER OUTSTANDING MEMORY WAS BLACKBURN'S LAST MATCH OF THE 1957-8 PROMOTION SEASON AT THE VALLEY. WE HAD TO WIN TO GO UP. IF CHARLTON WON — OR EVEN DREW — THEY WENT UP."

COME ON, REF — BLOW THAT BLOOMIN' WHISTLE !

A FELLOW-PRESTONIAN, FINNEY, SCORED SUPERB SOLO GOALS IN EACH GAME. I ONLY MISSED ONE OF ENGLAND'S NEXT 21 INTERNATIONALS.

R.BOND '65

"YOU CAN IMAGINE OUR DELIGHT AS WE RACED TO A 4-1 LEAD. BUT MID UNBEARABLE TENSION CHARLTON PULLED BACK TO 4-3! HOW WE HELD ON TO WIN PROMOTION I STILL DON'T KNOW...?"

CLAYTON WAS MADE SCAPEGOAT FOR A HEAVY ENGLAND DEFEAT BY YUGOSLAVIA THE SAME YEAR, AND DROPPED.

BUT HE RETURNED IN TIME TO HELP HIS COUNTRY HAMMER THE RUSSIANS AT WEMBLEY, AND THE FOLLOWING SEASON BECAME THE FIRST BLACKBURN PLAYER TO SKIPPER ENGLAND SINCE BOB CROMPTON.

I WOULD LOVE TO LEAD THE LADS TO VICTORY IN THE CUP-FINAL. WE NEARLY DID IT IN 1960, BUT WITH ONLY TEN MEN THE ODDS WERE TOO GREAT...

CLAYTON'S DEDICATION TO THE GAME HAS PAID HIM RICH DIVIDENDS, AND HIS REMARKABLE CONSISTENCY IN RECENT YEARS SHOULD HAVE WON HIM MORE HONOURS THAN IT HAS. MUCH OF ROVERS' SUCCESS HAS STEMMED FROM HIS EXAMPLE AND NEVER-SAY-DIE APPROACH.

Mike England
Central Defender
Born: Holywell, 2 December 1941

Recognised as one of the world's greatest centre halves, Mike England was more than simply a stopper with a strong tackle and dominating aerial ability. He was an outstanding defender with superb control and distribution skills capable of turning defence into attack with precision long balls to the forwards. Making his League debut in 1959, Mike's early first-team appearances for Blackburn were at full-back and wing half before he took over the mantle of Matt Woods in the centre of defence. Following a disastrous start to the 1965/66 season, he was switched to centre forward and immediately got on the scoresheet in the 4-1 away victory over Burnley. It was the club's second win in eleven starts but the revival was not sustained and the campaign ended in relegation. After making 165 appearances for Rovers, the club's prized asset was quickly rescued from the prospect of Second Division soccer by Spurs in a record deal for a defender. Honours followed at White Hart Lane with an FA Cup final win in 1967, the League Cup trophy in 1971 and 1973 and the UEFA Cup in 1972. Mike had deputised for the great John Charles in his first international for Wales after only three games at centre half for Blackburn and went on to win a total of 44 caps for his country, whom he later managed.

Joe Hulme
Winger
Born: Stafford, 26 August 1904

Rovers unearthed a major talent in 1924 when they paid the princely sum of £250 for non-League York City winger Joe Hulme. At Ewood Park, his electrifying pace marked him out as a future international. The highlight of his career at Blackburn was the FA Cup run of 1925 that was ended by Cardiff in the semi-final. The following season, having made 82 appearances for the club, Joe left for Arsenal managed by Herbert Chapman. An automatic choice at Highbury for the next ten years, Joe showed his class and settled in a forward line alongside all-time greats David Jack, Alex James, Charles Buchan and Cliff Bastin. Honours came quick and fast as the Gunners collected four League titles and appeared in three FA Cup finals. Joe also won 9 England soccer caps and embarked upon a successful cricket career with Middlesex, making twelve first-class centuries and scoring over 1,000 runs in a season on three occasions. Nearing the end of his playing days, Joe left Highbury, having collected 125 goals in 372 appearances, for Huddersfield, where he made only 10 appearances, the last of these on the fitting stage of Wembley, on the losing side against Preston in the 1938 FA Cup final.

Bryan Douglas
Winger/Midfield
Born: Blackburn, 27 May 1934

'The new Stanley Matthews' was a tag that Bryan Douglas had to live up to after replacing the old maestro in the England team. He was not blessed with the pace of Matthews or Burnley's John Connelly – a constant rival for the England number seven shirt – but his unhurried shuffling style and mesmerising trickery took him past defenders just as easily. Varying the usual winger's role of running and raiding, by holding and using the ball, this tactic was often misconstrued by impatient supporters. Refusing to aimlessly hit crosses into a packed penalty area, Bryan intelligently controlled the ball, while looking for an opportunity to open up the defence with a perfectly weighted pass, which in his early days would often raise a cry from the terraces of 'Get rid of it!'

'Duggie' made his international debut in 1957 and the same season helped Rovers to win promotion to the old First Division. His brilliance won him 36 international caps and Burnley's Jimmy McIlroy was not alone in recognising that Bryan's ball artistry was even more effective when he switched to midfield. A hometown discovery, Bryan was a one-club man, scoring over a century of goals in 438 appearances. He was a vital cog of the Rovers team that reached the FA Cup final in 1960, then an ever present in the England team during the 1962 World Cup finals in Chile. However, he was absent from the squad four years later, when in the same season England won the World Cup, Rovers were relegated and a string of injuries precluded one of the game's finest players from influencing the destiny of club or country. Rovers lost two great servants when Bryan bowed out of League soccer at the same time as Ronnie Clayton in 1969. The pair later conjured up memories of their great days together when they linked up at non-League Great Harwood.

Opposite: The life of Bryan, illustrated in March 1965.

Bobby Langton
Winger
Born: Ormskirk,
  8 September 1918

Enjoying an amazing career that straddled the Second World War, Bobby Langton made his League debut for Rovers in the promotion side which won the Second Division Championship in 1939. Having scored 14 goals in 37 appearances, the future looked bright for the exciting winger until Hitler's expansionist plans in Europe intervened and Bobby found himself turning out for Army teams for the next six years. His call-up also meant that he missed out on an appearance at Wembley in 1940 when Blackburn finished runners-up to West Ham in the first League War Cup final.

When League soccer resumed in 1946, Bobby's exhilarating form for Rovers won him the first of 11 international caps. Following Blackburn's relegation in 1948, he was transferred to Preston who had the immortal Tom Finney playing on the other flank, but a year later Bolton paid a club-record fee for Bobby's signature. The highlight of his stay at Burnden Park was the battle for the FA Cup against Blackpool in 1953, which ended in disappointment as the match was dominated by another great winger – Stanley Matthews. A few months later he returned to Ewood Park where his speed and ability to cut inside his marker for a crack at goal gradually faded, allowing his astute soccer brain to compensate for ageing legs. Pace was replaced by craft and guile which was utilised intelligently to penetrate opposing defences. His League career came to an end in 1956 having scored 74 goals in 262 appearances during two spells with Rovers where his electrifying wing play had made him a perennial crowd favourite.

Peter Dobing
Midfield/Forward
Born: Manchester,
    1 December 1938

Teenage goalscoring sensation Peter Dobing established himself in the Rovers side that won promotion to the top flight in 1958, notching 25 goals in 39 League and cup appearances. His career at Ewood Park had to be juggled with two years of National Service, but when he left for Manchester City in 1961, he was a mere twenty-two-years-old and had scored a remarkable 104 goals in 205 appearances, which included an FA Cup final. During the run to Wembley he scored in both sixth-round games against Burnley in an epic cup tie which was decided in a replay (see match report, pages 46-47). In 1963, he moved onto Stoke to take part in the revival triggered by the signing of Stanley Matthews. Spending ten years at the Victoria Ground, Peter gradually adapted his role from a strong-running striker to a deep-lying midfield schemer, combining vision with silky passing skills, while still retaining powerful shooting ability in his armoury. His midfield partners included former East Lancashire kingpins Jimmy McIlroy and Roy Vernon. He was an integral member of the Stoke team that won the Football League Cup in 1972, forming a potent playmaking partnership alongside England international George Eastham.

Although he enjoyed a long and successful career, Peter was overlooked for the full England side after winning 7 Under-23 caps and representing the Football League twice while at Ewood Park. When Peter retired he became one of an elite band of players to amass over 200 goals and 500 appearances in the Football League.

Roy Vernon
Midfield
Born: Prestatyn, 14 April 1937

Welsh wizard Roy Vernon was an enormously gifted inside forward whose creative play was allied to deadly finishing. Making his debut as an eighteen-year-old for Rovers in 1955, he got his opportunity as a direct result of manager Johnny Carey's youth policy dubbed the 'Carey Chicks'. A year later Roy won the first of 32 international caps for his country and was a member of the Welsh squad that acquitted itself so well by reaching the quarter-finals of the 1958 World Cup tournament held in Sweden.

When Johnny Carey moved to take over at Everton shortly after guiding Blackburn to promotion in 1958, Roy became unsettled and followed his mentor to Goodison Park in February 1960. In doing so he missed out on a FA Cup medal as Blackburn started their great run along the Wembley trail. Compensation came three seasons later when he captained the Toffees to the old First Division Championship. Roy clinched the title in the last game of the season with a glorious hat-trick in a 4-1 home win against Fulham and was the club's top scorer with 24 League goals. At Ewood Park, Roy had scored 52 goals in 144 League and cup appearances, an average which was improved to a goal every two games at Everton where he netted 101 goals in a total of 199 appearances. The twilight of his career was spent at Stoke City where he spent five years. In 1970, he teamed up with former Blackburn colleagues Ronnie Clayton and Bryan Douglas with non-League Great Harwood.

Opposite: A pictorial record of Roy Vernon's career in May 1967.

UH, OH... HERE HE COMES AGAIN...

A FREQUENT CHOICE FOR **WALES** OVER MANY YEARS, **ROY** HAS FAST REFLEXES AND DOESN'T NEED TO TEE UP HIS SHOT, HITTING IT FIRST TIME WITH EITHER FOOT...

ROY VERNON'S ASTUTE POSITIONAL PLAY AND DEADLY OPPORTUNISM HAVE TERRORISED DEFENCES FOR A DOZEN YEARS NOW. FANS AT **BLACKBURN, EVERTON** AND **STOKE** HAVE FOUND THAT HIS FIERCE SHOOTING COMPLETELY BELIES HIS LONG, LEAN APPEARANCE. GOALKEEPERS, TO THEIR COST, HAVE DISCOVERED THE SAME.

HIS PROMISE BEGAN TO SHOW AT EWOOD WHEN, IN THE COMPANY OF SUCH MEN AS **DOUGLAS** AND **CLAYTON**, HE HELPED **BLACKBURN** BACK INTO DIVISION ONE IN **1958**. THE LAST MATCH OF THAT SEASON, AT THE VALLEY WAS ONE **BLACKBURN** HAD TO WIN IN ORDER TO GO UP — **CHARLTON** ONLY NEEDED TO DRAW TO DO THE SAME.

ALREADY **VERNON** HAD PLAYED SEVERAL TIMES FOR **WALES**. ONE OF THOSE EARLY GAMES IN THE RED JERSEY WAS A WORLD CUP QUALIFIER AGAINST **CZECHOSLOVAKIA** IN CARDIFF IN **1957**. **VERNON** SHOT THE ONLY GOAL OF THE GAME, A MAGNIFICENT 25 YARDER, RIGHT OUT OF THE BLUE.

WE'RE THERE! PHEW, WHAT A RELIEF....

THERE IT IS! THE FINAL WHISTLE— AND WHAT A SCRAP! CHARLTON 3 BLACKBURN 4! DOBING (TWO), DOUGLAS AND VERNON THE SCORERS..... ROVERS WIN PROMOTION...

ROY FOLLOWED MANAGER **JOHNNY CAREY** FROM EWOOD TO **EVERTON** IN **1960**. THE FEE WAS £27,000 — A BARGAIN.

I HAD — AND STILL HAVE — THE GREATEST RESPECT FOR ROY. SO NATURALLY I MADE EVERY EFFORT TO SIGN HIM A SECOND TIME WHEN HE BECAME AVAILABLE....

GET READY TO CHALK ANOTHER ONE UP....

VERNON IS WELL-BALANCED, RUNS SMOOTHLY WITH DECEPTIVE SPEED, AND DRIBBLES CLEVERLY. AT GOODISON HE BECAME A PENALTY EXPERT, NOT FAILING ONCE IN NINE KICKS IN THE CHAMPIONSHIP SEASON 1962-3....

IN THE GAME WHICH CLINCHED THE TITLE, AGAINST **FULHAM**, HE SHOT A MEMORABLE HAT-TRICK, OF WHICH THE THIRD WAS A PARTICULARLY CLEVER CHIP FROM A NARROW ANGLE.

THE TEAM PLAYED SOME FANTASTIC FOOTBALL THAT DAY. I RECALL THAT THE GOODISON FANS WERE CHEERING NON-STOP THROUGHOUT THE SECOND HALF. I WAS LEADING SCORER IN THAT SEASON, AND IN FOUR OUT OF MY FIVE SEASONS AT EVERTON.....

VERNON WAS MADE MORE CONSPICUOUS BY HIS ABSENCE FROM **EVERTON** — HIS TRANSFER TO **STOKE** COST THE CLUB MUCH IN FINISHING POWER.

AFTER **JOHN RITCHIE** HAD LEFT THE POTTERIES LAST YEAR, **VERNON** WAS RESTORED TO LEAD THE ATTACK. MANAGER **TONY WADDINGTON** STILL RATES HIM AMONG THE LAND'S MOST DANGEROUS GOAL-GETTERS. WHAT OF **ROY VERNON**'S FUTURE? IF HE CAN KEEP CLEAR OF INJURIES MANY MORE GOALS, SURELY.

Danny Shea

Midfield/Forward
Born: Wapping,
  6 November 1887

Blackburn Rovers broke the British transfer record and paid the first-ever £2,000 fee to lure Danny Shea from non-League club West Ham in 1913. The 'Wapping Wizard' justified the high price tag as his unique ability as a creative schemer and prolific scorer made him the outstanding player in a star-studded forward line which included England internationals Jock Simpson, Eddie Latherton and Joe Hodkinson.

As Rovers claimed the League Championship in 1914, Danny hit two hat-tricks and he went one better against Liverpool, scoring four. He ended the campaign as the club's top scorer with 30 goals in 39 League and cup matches – a staggering total considering his main role was that of playmaker. His dazzling form also won him 2 international caps before war intervened at the height of his playing career. Upon the resumption of League soccer in 1919, Danny played in two Victory Internationals, then midway through the season moved back to West Ham, having collected 64 goals in 125 appearances for Blackburn. Measuring only 5' 6" tall, Danny had set out on his playing career as a centre forward, but his lack of inches made managers reluctant to play him there. Nevertheless, his abundant skill enabled him to become an inside forward of the highest class, while retaining a sharp eye for goal!

Alan Shearer
Striker
Born: Newcastle,
   13 August 1970

The kingpin of the 'Walker Revolution', Alan Shearer's transfer to Blackburn caused a sensation when manager Kenny Dalglish paid a British-record fee of £3.25 million for the forward's signature in 1992. Alan had established himself as an England international with Southampton, but at Blackburn he was to fully realise his potential and become recognised as a world-class striker. Alan announced his arrival with two stunning rocket-powered goals on his debut at Crystal Palace. Going on to became the first player to score 100 Premiership goals, he notched 30 goals in three successive seasons, amassing 130 goals in only 171 appearances. This record was achieved after overcoming a career-threatening cruciate ligament injury which occurred during his first season at Ewood Park. Battling back to fitness, the goals continued to flow as the Football Writers' Association voted him Player of the Year in 1994 and his fellow professionals bestowed the PFA Player of the Year award the following season when he sealed Blackburn's comeback to the big time by captaining the side to the ultimate domestic prize – the Premiership title.

Possessed of a mix of power and goalscoring ability reminiscent of great old-fashioned England centre forwards like Tommy Lawton and Nat Lofthouse, Alan attracted a world-record bid of £15million from his native Newcastle in 1996 where he continued to revitalise the club's fortunes after retiring from international soccer with 30 goals in 63 England matches at the end of Euro 2000. Deservedly, his name is among the elite band of players who have been inducted to the FA Premier League Hall of Fame.

Derek Dougan
Striker
Born: Belfast, 20 January 1938

Mercurial Irishman Derek Dougan made his presence felt at Ewood Park where the gangling old-fashioned centre forward scored 34 goals in 76 entertaining appearances for Blackburn Rovers. A controversial character who sported skinhead and Mohican hairstyles long before David Beckham was born, the 'Doog' had the personality to draw crowds even though his attention-seeking behaviour could be a little over the top on occasions. One such incident occurred during the FA Cup sixth-round replay against Burnley in 1960 (see match report, pages 148-149). Shortly before half-time Derek left the field for treatment. During the interval, he recovered and was fit to resume, but as the teams lined up for the restart without him, the 'Doog' suddenly limped back into view to milk the relieved applause of the supporters. The love affair with Rovers, which had begun when he was signed from Portsmouth in March 1959, ended when Derek chose to post a letter requesting a transfer on the day of the 1960 FA Cup final. The colourful striker then pronounced himself recovered from injury but as the game progressed it became patently obvious that he was not fully fit as Rovers struggled in vain to overcome the loss of Wembley 'hoodoo' victim Dave Whelan. Dougan won a total of 43 caps for Northern Ireland and served several clubs. His best spell came during his final move to Wolves who after gaining promotion to the top flight in 1967, became UEFA Cup finalists in 1972 and League Cup winners in 1974. After making a career of clashing with authority, this rebellious character emerged as an establishment figure himself as an innovative chairman of the PFA.

Blackburn Rovers Dream Team

Fred Else

Bob Crompton   Ron Clayton   Mike England   Bill Eckersley

Joe Hulme   Bryan Douglas   Roy Vernon   Bobby Langton

Alan Shearer   Danny Shea

Subs: Herbie Arthur, Jimmy Forrest, Harry Healless, Peter Dobing, Derek Dougan

The immortal Bob Crompton takes charge of the Blackburn Rovers 'dream team' and lines up in a formidable back four alongside dominant central defenders Ronnie Clayton and Mike England together with tenacious left-back Bill Eckersley. Anything that gets past the defensive wall will be dealt with by the capable hands of 'keeper Fred Else – the only uncapped player in the starting line-up. In midfield, a sparkling combination of Bryan Douglas and Roy Vernon will link up with virtuoso Danny Shea to create opportunities for flying goalscoring wingers Joe Hulme and Bobby Langton. Waiting upfront for the final delivery is predator supreme Alan Shearer. Manager Bob Crompton can make tactical switches where necessary by calling upon the services of a talented subs bench which includes goalkeeper Herbie Arthur, defenders Jimmy Forrest and Harry Healless; midfield Peter Dobing and striker Derek

Dougan. With all the many great players that have turned out for Burnley and Blackburn Rovers to choose from, these squads will not meet with universal approval from other would-be selectors, but they represent the individuals that have captured my imagination. With proven capability of performing at the highest level, these soccer legends would provide a East Lancashire derby to remember. If only they could be brought together at the peak of their ability by Old Father Time.

Ronnie Clayton, Roy Vernon and Bryan Douglas get the 'thumbs-up' to line up in the fantasy team.

Blackburn Rovers Dream Team

Fred Else

Bob Crompton

Ron Clayton

Mike England

Bill Eckersley

Joe Hulme

Bryan Douglas

Roy Vernon

Bobby Langton

Alan Shearer

Danny Shea

7

FINAL SCORE

The East Lancashire Derby Score 1882-2004

Cup Derby Results

Pre-League Derby Friendlies

League Derby Results

Lancashire Hotshots – Leading League Goalscorers

50 Great East Lancashire Servants

THE EAST LANCASHIRE DERBY SCORE 1882-2004

PRE-LEAGUE	P	W	D	L	F	A
BLACKBURN	14	5	2	7	25	26
BURNLEY	14	7	2	5	26	25

LEAGUE	P	W	D	L	F	A
BLACKBURN	82	36	13	33	156	141
BURNLEY	82	33	13	36	141	156

TEST MATCHES	P	W	D	L	F	A
BLACKBURN	2	0	0	2	1	5
BURNLEY	2	2	0	0	5	1

WARTIME MATCHES	P	W	D	L	F	A
BLACKBURN	37	13	7	17	61	77
BURNLEY	37	17	7	13	77	61

LANCASHIRE CUP	P	W	D	L	F	A
BLACKBURN	7	3	3	1	10	6
BURNLEY	7	1	3	3	6	10

FA CUP	P	W	D	L	F	A
BLACKBURN	5	2	1	2	9	7
BURNLEY	5	2	1	2	7	9

ANGLO-SCOTS CUP	P	W	D	L	F	A
BLACKBURN	4	0	3	1	5	6
BURNLEY	4	1	3	0	6	5

MANX CUP	P	W	D	L	F	A
BLACKBURN	5	3	1	1	8	4
BURNLEY	5	1	1	3	4	8

TOTAL	P	W	D	L	F	A
BLACKBURN	156	62	30	64	275	272
BURNLEY	156	64	30	62	272	275

CUP DERBY RESULTS

LANCASHIRE CUP

1889/90	BURNLEY 2	BLACKBURN 0	FINAL
1900/01	BLACKBURN 1	BURNLEY 0	FINAL
1901/02	BLACKBURN 1	BURNLEY 0	FINAL
1910/11	BLACKBURN 1	BURNLEY 1	FINAL
	BLACKBURN 2	BURNLEY 2	REPLAY
	BLACKBURN 0	BURNLEY 0	2nd REPLAY
	BLACKBURN 2	BURNLEY 1	3rd REPLAY

FA CUP DERBIES

8 MARCH 1913	BLACKBURN 0	BURNLEY 1	SIXTH ROUND
8 MARCH 1952	BLACKBURN 3	BURNLEY 1	SIXTH ROUND
24 JANUARY 1959	BLACKBURN 0	BURNLEY 0	ABANDONED
28 JANUARY 1959	BLACKBURN 1	BURNLEY 2	FOURTH ROUND
12 MARCH 1960	BURNLEY 3	BLACKBURN 3	SIXTH ROUND
16 MARCH 1960	BLACKBURN 2	BURNLEY 0	SIXTH ROUND REPLAY

ANGLO-SCOTTISH CUP DERBIES

7 AUGUST 1976	BLACKBURN 1	BURNLEY 1	PRELIMINARY GROUP
2 AUGUST 1977	BURNLEY 2	BLACKBURN 1	PRELIMINARY GROUP
12 AUGUST 1978	BLACKBURN 1	BURNLEY 1	PRELIMINARY GROUP
4 AUGUST 1979	BLACKBURN 2	BURNLEY 2	PRELIMINARY GROUP

LANCASHIRE-MANX CUP DERBIES

16 AUGUST 1983	BURNLEY 1	BLACKBURN 1	GROUP MATCH
13 AUGUST 1985	BLACKBURN 1	BURNLEY 0	FINAL
4 AUGUST 1987	BURNLEY 2	BLACKBURN 1	GROUP MATCH
9 AUGUST 1988	BURNLEY 1	BLACKBURN 3	GROUP MATCH
8 AUGUST 1989	BURNLEY 0	BLACKBURN 2	GROUP MATCH

PRE-LEAGUE DERBY FRIENDLIES

21 OCTOBER 1882	BURNLEY 0	BLACKBURN 10
27 SEPTEMBER 1884	BURNLEY 2	BLACKBURN 4
23 MARCH 1885	BURNLEY 5	BLACKBURN 1
3 OCTOBER 1885	BLACKBURN 2	BURNLEY 2
19 OCTOBER 1885	BURNLEY 1	BLACKBURN 1
14 DECEMBER 1885	BLACKBURN 0	BURNLEY 2
6 FEBRUARY 1886	BURNLEY 1	BLACKBURN 0
15 NOVEMBER 1886	BURNLEY 0	BLACKBURN 1
22 JANUARY 1886	BURNLEY 4	BLACKBURN 0
24 JANUARY 1887	BLACKBURN 1	BURNLEY 0
2 APRIL 1887	BLACKBURN 0	BURNLEY 2
18 APRIL 1887	BURNLEY 2	BLACKBURN 1
10 SEPTEMBER 1887	BLACKBURN 3	BURNLEY 2
28 APRIL 1888	BURNLEY 3	BLACKBURN 1

LEAGUE DERBY RESULTS

SEASON	LEAGUE	DATE	RESULT and final position
1888/89	FL	3 NOVEMBER	BURNLEY 1 BLACKBURN 7
			Blackburn 4th
	FL	4 FEBRUARY	BLACKBURN 4 BURNLEY 0
			Burnley 9th, Re-elected
1889/90	FL	26 OCTOBER	BLACKBURN 7 BURNLEY 1
			Blackburn 3rd
	FL	22 FEBRUARY	BURNLEY 1 BLACKBURN 2
			Burnley 11th Re-elected
1890/91	FL	18 OCTOBER	BURNLEY 1 BLACKBURN 6
			Blackburn 6th
	FL	22 NOVEMBER	BLACKBURN 5 BURNLEY 2
			Burnley 8th
1891/92	FL	26 SEPTEMBER	BLACKBURN 3 BURNLEY 3
			Burnley 7th
	FL	12 DECEMBER	BURNLEY 3 BLACKBURN 1
			Blackburn 9th
1892/93	FL FIRST DIVISION	3 DECEMBER	BURNLEY 0 BLACKBURN 0
			Burnley 6th
	FL FIRST DIVISION	17 DECEMBER	BLACKBURN 2 BURNLEY 0
			Blackburn 9th
1893/94	FL FIRST DIVISION	18 NOVEMBER	BLACKBURN 3 BURNLEY 2
			Blackburn 4th
	FL FIRST DIVISION	23 DECEMBER	BURNLEY 1 BLACKBURN 0
			Burnley 5th
1894/95	FL FIRST DIVISION	17 NOVEMBER	BLACKBURN 1 BURNLEY 0
			Blackburn 5th
	FL FIRST DIVISION	12 JANUARY	BURNLEY 2 BLACKBURN 1
			Burnley 9th
1895/96	FL FIRST DIVISION	5 OCTOBER	BLACKBURN 1 BURNLEY 0
			Blackburn 8th
	FL FIRST DIVISION	13 APRIL	BURNLEY 6 BLACKBURN 0
			Burnley 10th
1896/97	FL FIRST DIVISION	3 OCTOBER	BLACKBURN 3 BURNLEY 2
			Blackburn 14th
	FL FIRST DIVISION	7 NOVEMBER	BURNLEY 0 BLACKBURN 1
			Burnley 16th, relegated after a play-off system of Test Matches
1897/98	TEST MATCH	21 APRIL	BLACKBURN 1 BURNLEY 3
			Blackburn 14th (FIRST DIVISION)
	TEST MATCH	23 APRIL	BURNLEY 2 BLACKBURN 0
			Burnley 1st (SECOND DIVISION)

Burnley promoted – Blackburn are relegated then reinstated to the First Division when the football league is enlarged to eighteen clubs in each division.

1898/99	FL FIRST DIVISION	26 NOVEMBER	BURNLEY 2 BLACKBURN 1
			Burnley 3rd
	FL FIRST DIVISION	26 DECEMBER	BLACKBURN 0 BURNLEY 2
			Blackburn 6th

1899/00	FL FIRST DIVISION	7 OCTOBER	BURNLEY 1 BLACKBURN 0
			Blackburn 14th
	FL FIRST DIVISION	1 JANUARY	BLACKBURN 2 BURNLEY 0
			Burnley 17th, relegated
1913/14	FL FIRST DIVISION	8 SEPTEMBER	BURNLEY 1 BLACKBURN 2
			Blackburn 1st
	FL FIRST DIVISION	1 JANUARY	BLACKBURN 0 BURNLEY 0
			Burnley 12th
1914/15	FL FIRST DIVISION	28 NOVEMBER	BLACKBURN 6 BURNLEY 0
			Blackburn 3rd
	FL FIRST DIVISION	3 APRIL	BURNLEY 3 BLACKBURN 2
			Burnley 4th
1919/20	FL FIRST DIVISION	13 SEPTEMBER	BLACKBURN 2 BURNLEY 3
			Burnley 2nd
	FL FIRST DIVISION	20 SEPTEMBER	BURNLEY 3 BLACKBURN 1
			Blackburn 20th
1920/21	FL FIRST DIVISION	15 JANUARY	BURNLEY 4 BLACKBURN 1
			Burnley 1st
	FL FIRST DIVISION	22 JANUARY	BLACKBURN 1 BURNLEY 3
			Blackburn 11th
1921/22	FL FIRST DIVISION	4 FEBRUARY	BLACKBURN 3 BURNLEY 2
			Burnley 3rd
	FL FIRST DIVISION	11 FEBRUARY	BURNLEY 1 BLACKBURN 2
			Blackburn 15th
1922/23	FL FIRST DIVISION	21 OCTOBER	BURNLEY 3 BLACKBURN 1
			Blackburn 14th
	FL FIRST DIVISION	28 OCTOBER	BLACKBURN 2 BURNLEY 1
			Burnley 15th
1923/24	FL FIRST DIVISION	3 NOVEMBER	BLACKBURN 1 BURNLEY 1
			Blackburn 8th
	FL FIRST DIVISION	10 NOVEMBER	BURNLEY 1 BLACKBURN 2
			Burnley 17th
1924/25	FL FIRST DIVISION	13 SEPTEMBER	BURNLEY 3 BLACKBURN 5
			Blackburn 16th
	FL FIRST DIVISION	17 JANUARY	BLACKBURN 0 BURNLEY 3
			Burnley 19th
1925/26	FL FIRST DIVISION	31 OCTOBER	BURNLEY 1 BLACKBURN 3
			Blackburn 12th
	FL FIRST DIVISION	13 MARCH	BLACKBURN 6 BURNLEY 3
			Burnley 20th
1926/27	FL FIRST DIVISION	16 OCTOBER	BLACKBURN 1 BURNLEY 5
			Burnley 5th
	FL FIRST DIVISION	5 MARCH	BURNLEY 3 BLACKBURN 1
			Blackburn 18th
1927/28	FL FIRST DIVISION	27 AUGUST	BLACKBURN 2 BURNLEY 1
			Blackburn 12th
	FL FIRST DIVISION	31 DECEMBER	BURNLEY 3 BLACKBURN 1
			Burnley 19th
1928/29	FL FIRST DIVISION	20 OCTOBER	BURNLEY 2 BLACKBURN 2
			Blackburn 7th

	FL FIRST DIVISION	2 MAY	BLACKBURN 1 BURNLEY 1
			Burnley 19th
1929/30	FL FIRST DIVISION	9 NOVEMBER	BLACKBURN 8 BURNLEY 3
			Blackburn 6th
	FL FIRST DIVISION	15 MARCH	BURNLEY 3 BLACKBURN 2
			Burnley 21st, relegated
1936/37	FL SECOND DIVISION	24 OCTOBER	BURNLEY 0 BLACKBURN 0
			Blackburn 12th
	FL SECOND DIVISION	27 FEBRUARY	BLACKBURN 3 BURNLEY 1
			Burnley 13th
1937/38	FL SECOND DIVISION	11 DECEMBER	BLACKBURN 3 BURNLEY 3
			Burnley 6th
	FL SECOND DIVISION	23 APRIL	BURNLEY 3 BLACKBURN 1
			Blackburn 16th
1938/39	FL SECOND DIVISION	15 OCTOBER	BURNLEY 3 BLACKBURN 2
			Blackburn 1st, promoted
	FL SECOND DIVISION	18 FEBRUARY	BLACKBURN 1 BURNLEY 0
			Burnley 14th
1947/48	FL FIRST DIVISION	18 OCTOBER	BLACKBURN 1 BURNLEY 2
			Burnley 3rd
	FL FIRST DIVISION	6 MARCH	BURNLEY 0 BLACKBURN 0
			Blackburn 21st, relegated
1958/59	FL FIRST DIVISION	18 OCTOBER	BURNLEY 0 BLACKBURN 0
			Burnley 7th
	FL FIRST DIVISION	28 JANUARY	BLACKBURN 1 BURNLEY 2
			Blackburn 10th
1959/60	FL FIRST DIVISION	17 OCTOBER	BLACKBURN 3 BURNLEY 2
			Burnley 1st
	FL FIRST DIVISION	5 MARCH	BURNLEY 1 BLACKBURN 0
			Blackburn 17th
1960/61	FL FIRST DIVISION	8 OCTOBER	BLACKBURN 1 BURNLEY 4
			Burnley 4th
	FL FIRST DIVISION	25 FEBRUARY	BURNLEY 1 BLACKBURN 1
			Blackburn 8th
1961/62	FL FIRST DIVISION	24 FEBRUARY	BLACKBURN 2 BURNLEY 1
			Burnley 2nd
	FL FIRST DIVISION	17 APRIL	BURNLEY 0 BLACKBURN 0
			Blackburn 16th
1962/63	FL FIRST DIVISION	6 OCTOBER	BLACKBURN 2 BURNLEY 3
			Burnley 3rd
	FL FIRST DIVISION	2 APRIL	BURNLEY 1 BLACKBURN 0
			Blackburn 11th
1963/64	FL FIRST DIVISION	1 OCTOBER	BURNLEY 3 BLACKBURN 0
			Blackburn 7th
	FL FIRST DIVISION	19 0CTOBER	BLACKBURN 1 BURNLEY 2
			Burnley 9th
1964/65	FL FIRST DIVISION	10 OCTOBER	BURNLEY 1 BLACKBURN 1
			Blackburn 10th

	FL FIRST DIVISION	24 FEBRUARY	BLACKBURN 1 BURNLEY 4
			Burnley 12th
1965/66	FL FIRST DIVISION	9 OCTOBER	BURNLEY 1 BLACKBURN 4
			Burnley 3rd
	FL FIRST DIVISION	1 JANUARY	BLACKBURN 0 BURNLEY 2
			Blackburn 22nd, relegated
1976/77	FL SECOND DIVISION	27 DECEMBER	BLACKBURN 2 BURNLEY 2
			Blackburn 12th
	FL SECOND DIVISION	8 APRIL	BURNLEY 3 BLACKBURN 1
			Burnley 16th
1977/78	FL SECOND DIVISION	26 DECEMBER	BURNLEY 2 BLACKBURN 3
			Blackburn 5th
	FL SECOND DIVISION	27 MARCH	BLACKBURN 0 BURNLEY 1
			Burnley 11th
1978/79	FL SECOND DIVISION	26 DECEMBER	BURNLEY 2 BLACKBURN 1
			Burnley 13th
	FL SECOND DIVISION	14 APRIL	BLACKBURN 1 BURNLEY 2
			Blackburn 22nd, relegated
1982/83	FL SECOND DIVISION	27 DECEMBER	BURNLEY 0 BLACKBURN 1
			Blackburn 11th
	FL SECOND DIVISION	4 APRIL	BLACKBURN 2 BURNLEY 1
			Burnley 21st, relegated
2000/01	FL DIVISION ONE	17 DECEMBER	BURNLEY 0 BLACKBURN 2
			Blackburn 2nd, promoted
	FL DIVISION ONE	1 APRIL	BLACKBURN 5 BURNLEY 0
			Burnley 7th

LANCASHIRE HOTSHOTS – LEADING LEAGUE GOALSCORERS

SEASON	BLACKBURN	TOTAL	BURNLEY	TOTAL
1888/89	JACK SOUTHWORTH	17	ALEX BRADY	7
1889/90	JACK SOUTHWORTH	22	BOB HARESNAPE/	
			CLAUDE LAMBIE	5
1890/91	JACK SOUTHWORTH	26	CLAUDE LAMBIE	16
1891/92	JACK SOUTHWORTH	22	TOM NICOL	17
1892/93	BILL SAWERS	11	BILL BOWES/	
			BOB BUCHANAN	8
1893/94	HARRY CHIPPENDALE	14	PETER TURNBULL	15
1894/95	HARRY CHIPPENDALE	12	TOM NICOL	11
1895/96	PETER TURNBULL/			
	HARRY CHIPPENDALE	7	HUGH ROBERTSON	10
1896/97	JOHN WILKIE	7	BILL BOWES	11
1897/98	JOHN PROUDFOOT	9	JIMMY ROSS	23
1898/99	DAN HURST	14	WILF TOMAN	11
1899/00	FRED BLACKBURN	9	EDGAR CHADWICK	10
1900/01	ARNOLD WHITTAKER	8	BILL BOWES/	
			BILL JENKINSON	9

SEASON	BLACKBURN	TOTAL	BURNLEY	TOTAL
1901/02	JACK DEWHURST	16	CORNELIUS HOGAN	10
1902/03	ARNOLD WHITTAKER	10	CORNELIUS HOGAN	7
1903/04	LIONEL WATSON	14	DUGALD McFARLANE	8
1904/05	ADAM BOWMAN	12	DUGALD McFARLANE	14
1905/06	ADAM BOWMAN	15	DUGALD McFARLANE	10
1906/07	JACK MARTIN	17	DICK SMITH	17
1907/08	BILLY DAVIES	11	DICK SMITH	24
1908/09	BILLY DAVIES	19	DICK SMITH	13
1909/10	WATTIE AITKENHEAD	12	BEN GREEN	18
1910/11	BILLY DAVIES	17	BEN GREEN	11
1911/12	WATTIE AITKENHEAD	15	BERT FREEMAN	32
1912/13	EDDIE LATHERTON	14	BERT FREEMAN	31
1913/14	DANNY SHEA	28	BERT FREEMAN	16
1914/15	PERCY DAWSON	20	TEDDY HODGSON	19
1919/20	ERNIE HAWKSWORTH	17	BERT FREEMAN	12
1920/21	PERCY DAWSON	17	JOE ANDERSON	25
1921/22	PERCY DAWSON	12	JOE ANDERSON	20
1922/23	JOCK McKAY	12	BOB KELLY	17
1923/24	TED HARPER	18	GEORGE BEEL	19
1924/25	JOCK McKAY/			
	JOHN McINTYRE	12	TOM ROBERTS	15
1925/26	TED HARPER	43	LOUIS PAGE	26
1926/27	TED HARPER	35	GEORGE BEEL	24
1927/28	TOM MITCHELL	15	GEORGE BEEL	35
1928/29	JACK ROSCAMP	16	GEORGE BEEL	30
1929/30	CLARRIE BOURTON	21	LOUIS PAGE	15
1930/31	LES BRUTON	18	GEORGE BEEL	25
1931/32	ERNIE THOMPSON	21	GEORGE BEEL	11
1932/33	ERNIE THOMPSON	17	TOM JONES	16
1933/34	TED HARPER/JACK BRUTON	15	CECIL SMITH	17
1934/35	JACK BRUTON/			
	ERNIE THOMPSON	18	GEORGE BROWN	21
1935/36	ERNIE THOMPSON	15	CECIL SMITH	10
1936/37	JACK BRUTON	16	CHARLIE FLETCHER	12
1937/38	LEN BUTT	20	BOB BROCKLEBANK	14
1938/39	ALBERT CLARKE	21	JIM CLAYTON	10
1946/47	JACK SMITH	12	HARRY POTTS	15
1947/48	LES GRAHAM	15	HARRY POTTS	14
1948/49	DENNIS WESTCOTT	21	JACK CHEW	11
1949/50	DENNIS WESTCOTT	16	HARRY POTTS	11
1950/51	LES GRAHAM	13	BILL HOLDEN	12
1951/52	EDDIE QUIGLEY	11	BILL MORRIS	18
1952/53	EDDIE QUIGLEY	18	BILL HOLDEN	22
1953/54	TOMMY BRIGGS	32	BILLY GRAY	19
1954/55	TOMMY BRIGGS	33	BILL HOLDEN	15
1955/56	TOMMY BRIGGS	31	PETER McKAY	25
1956/57	TOMMY BRIGGS	32	JIMMY McILROY	13
1957/58	PETER DOBING	20	JIMMY McILROY	16

SEASON	BLACKBURN	TOTAL	BURNLEY	TOTAL
1958/59	PETER DOBING	24	RAY POINTER	27
1959/60	PETER DOBING	18	JOHN CONNELLY	20
1960/61	PETER DOBING	18	JIMMY ROBSON	25
1961/62	IAN LAWTHER	14	RAY POINTER	25
1962/63	FRED PICKERING	23	ANDY LOCHHEAD	19
1963/64	ANDY McEVOY	32	ANDY LOCHHEAD	11
1964/65	ANDY McEVOY	29	WILLIE IRVINE	22
1965/66	ANDY McEVOY	10	WILLIE IRVINE	29
1966/67	JOHN CONNELLY	11	ANDY LOCHHEAD	18
1967/68	MIKE FERGUSON	8	FRANK CASPER	14
1968/69	MALCOLM DARLING	10	FRANK CASPER	13
1969/70	DON MARTIN	13	STEVE KINDON	17
1970/71	BRYAN CONLON	6	ERIC PROBERT	5
1971/72	TONY FIELD	17	FRANK CASPER	18
1972/73	TONY FIELD	17	PAUL FLETCHER	15
1973/74	TONY FIELD	11	PAUL FLETCHER	13
1974/75	DON MARTIN	15	LEIGHTON JAMES	16
1975/76	KEN BEAMISH/			
	TONY PARKES	7	RAY HANKIN	13
1976/77	BOBBY SVARC	10	PETER NOBLE	13
1977/78	NOEL BROTHERSTON	11	STEVE KINDON	12
1978/79	SIMON GARNER	8	PETER NOBLE	14
1979/80	ANDY CRAWFORD	18	BILLY HAMILTON	7
1980/81	KEVIN STONEHOUSE	10	STEVE TAYLOR	16
1981/82	SIMON GARNER	14	BILLY HAMILTON	11
1982/83	SIMON GARNER	22	BILLY HAMILTON	13
1983/84	SIMON GARNER	19	BILLY HAMILTON	18
1984/85	CHRIS THOMPSON	15	WAYNE BIGGINS	18
1985/86	SIMON GARNER	12	ALAN TAYLOR	16
1986/87	SIMON BARKER	11	LEIGHTON JAMES	10
1987/88	SIMON GARNER	14	GEORGE OGHANI	14
1988/89	SIMON GARNER	20	BRENDAN O'CONNELL	13
1989/90	SIMON GARNER	18	RON FUTCHER/	
			WINSTON WHITE	7
1990/91	FRANK STAPLETON	10	RON FUTCHER	18
1991/92	DAVID SPEEDIE	23	MIKE CONROY	24
1992/93	ALAN SHEARER	16	ADRIAN HEATH	19
1993/94	ALAN SHEARER	31	DAVID EYRES	19
1994/95	ALAN SHEARER	34	DAVID EYRES	8
1995/96	ALAN SHEARER	31	KURT NOGAN	20
1996/97	CHRIS SUTTON	11	PAUL BARNES	24
1997/98	CHRIS SUTTON	18	ANDY COOKE	16
1998/99	KEVIN GALLACHER	5	ANDY PAYTON	20
1999/00	LEE CARSLEY	10	ANDY PAYTON	27
2000/01	MATT JANSEN	23	ANDY PAYTON	9
2001/02	MATT JANSEN	16	GARETH TAYLOR	16
2002/03	ANDY COLE/			
	DWIGHT YORKE	13	GARETH TAYLOR	16
2003/04	ANDY COLE	11	ROBBIE BLAKE	19

FIFTY GREAT SERVANTS OF EAST LANCASHIRE CLUBS

First-team records including substitute appearances

BURNLEY	TOTAL	BLACKBURN ROVERS	TOTAL
JERRY DAWSON	569	DEREK FAZACKERLEY	689
ALAN STEVENSON	543	RON CLAYTON	665
JOHN ANGUS	521	BOB CROMPTON	608
MARTIN DOBSON	499	SIMON GARNER	570
JIMMY McILROY	497	BOB PRYDE	525
JIMMY ADAMSON	486	BRYAN DOUGLAS	503
TOMMY CUMMINGS	479	BILLY BRADSHAW	457
BRIAN MILLER	455	STUART METCALFE	451
FRED BARRON	423	GLENN KEELEY	430
LEIGHTON JAMES	403	ARNOLD WHITESIDE	416
GEORGE WATERFIELD	394	TONY PARKES	409
ADAM BLACKLAW	383	COLIN HENDRY	408
BILLY WATSON	380	HARRY HEALLESS	399
JIM THOMSON	363	NOEL BROTHERSTON	381
DEREK SCOTT	364	ERIC BELL	370
COLIN WALDRON	356	KEITH NEWTON	357
JOE TAYLOR	352	JACK BRUTON	345
PAUL FLETCHER	352	WALTER CROOK	350
BRIAN PILKINGTON	340	JIM BRANAGAN	338
GEORGE BEEL	337	ALBERT WALMSLEY	335
ALEX ELDER	330	TERRY GENNOE	334
GORDON HARRIS	313	ARTHUR COWELL	321
BILLY RODAWAY	305	JASON WILCOX	313
PETER NOBLE	300	MICK McGRATH	312
BOB KELLY	299	MICK RATHBONE	310